WITHDRAWN

More praise for
What We Talk About When We Talk About Rape

"The right to our own bodies is the first step in any democracy and, by that measure, women in general—especially those of us also de-valued by race, caste, or class—are still subject to an intimate dictatorship. Read the personal stories in *What We Talk About When We Talk About Rape* and see how far we have come—and have yet to go."

—Gloria Steinem

"Both hard to read and an amazing, vital read, *What We Talk About When We Talk About Rape* is the exact book we all need right now. Abdulali is a brilliant and beautiful writer, filled with empathy, and she is a thought leader for our generation."

—Alyssa Mastromonaco, author of *Who Thought This Was a Good Idea?*, co-host of *Hysteria* podcast, and former White House deputy chief of staff

"*What We Talk About When We Talk About Rape* places the American #MeToo movement in a global context. Sohaila Abdulali takes us from the U.S. to India, South Africa, Mexico, Kuwait, and other countries, providing examples that illustrate both the intense particularity and the infuriating similarities of sexual violence around the globe. The book is courageous, angry, compassionate, informative, hopeful, and wise."

—Elizabeth A. Armstrong, professor of sociology, University of Michigan

"Know this: the shock is not that Abdulali speaks frankly about rape. The shock is not that she interrogates the content, and limits, of our public discourses about rape culture with candor and warmth, with cool precision and justified rage, with wisdom and, yes, humor. The shock is that there are not more books like this. Read it, and do not stop talking."

—Sarah Krasnostein, author of *The Trauma Cleaner*

"Such a lot of insight in this book. I wish I had written it. The more we talk, the more we learn. The more we learn, the more we can change. Read this book and be part of the change."

—Una, author of *Becoming Unbecoming*

"This is a vital, eye-opening exploration of a crime which affects too many of us, in often unspoken but always life-changing ways. Sohaila Abdulali's voice is an honest, wry, engaging, and very human testament to the survivor's voice as a necessary tool for change. It is filled with truths that will resonate with millions of us—and educate millions more."

—Winnie M. Li, author of *Dark Chapter*

What We Talk About When We Talk About RAPE

Sohaila
Abdulali

THE
NEW
PRESS

NEW YORK
LONDON

© 2018 by Sohaila Abdulali
All rights reserved.
No part of this book may be reproduced, in any form,
without written permission from the publisher.

Requests for permission to reproduce selections from this book
should be mailed to: Permissions Department,
The New Press, 120 Wall Street, 31st floor, New York, NY 10005.

Every attempt has been made to obtain the necessary permissions for
use of copyrighted material. For a full permissions list,
see pages 225–26.
If there have been any omissions, we apologise and will be pleased to
make appropriate acknowledgement in any future edition.

First published in Great Britain by Myriad Editions,
an imprint of New Internationalist Publications, 2018
Published in the United States by The New Press, New York, 2018
Distributed by Two Rivers Distribution

ISBN 978-1-62097-475-9 (ebook)

LIBRARY OF CONGRESS CATALOGING-IN-PUBLICATION DATA

Names: Abdulali, Sohaila, author.
Title: What we talk about when we talk about rape / Sohaila Abdulali.
Description: New York : New Press, [2018] | Includes bibliographical
references and index.
Identifiers: LCCN 2018034364 | ISBN 9781620974735 (hardcover : alk.
paper) | ISBN 9781620974742 (pbk. : alk. paper)
Subjects: LCSH: Rape. | Rape victims.
Classification: LCC HV6558 .A295 2018 | DDC 364.15/32—dc23
LC record available at https://lccn.loc.gov/2018034364

The New Press publishes books that promote and enrich public
discussion and understanding of the issues vital to our democracy
and to a more equitable world. These books are made possible by
the enthusiasm of our readers; the support of a committed group of
donors, large and small; the collaboration of our many partners in the
independent media and the not-for-profit sector; booksellers, who often
hand-sell New Press books; librarians; and above all by our authors.

www.thenewpress.com

Composition by WatchWord Editorial Services, London
This book was set in Palatino

Printed in the United States of America

2 4 6 8 10 9 7 5 3 1

For Samara, Aidan, and Rafe
Teatime forever

Contents

Disclaimer

I've used anecdotes from many people's lives, including my own. I haven't made up anything, but I have taken some liberties with names, places, etcetera, to respect people's privacy. In some cases I have used pseudonyms. Every quote in this book is real, but, if I say A's uncle said it, it might actually be B's father. It's all true, but it's not all necessarily true in exactly the order I tell you it is.

1

Introduction

The light was draining out of the room, going back through the window where it had come from.

— Raymond Carver, "Beginners" (originally "What We Talk About When We Talk About Love")

RAPE DRAINS the light. Like J.K. Rowling's fantastically terrifying Dementors, it sucks joy. And, along with draining the light from victims' lives, it tends to drain the light from sensible conversation. Discussions about rape are so often irrational, and sometimes outright bizarre. It's the only crime to which people respond by wanting to lock up the victims. It's the only crime that is so bad that victims are supposed to be destroyed beyond repair by it, but simultaneously not so bad that the men who do it should be treated like other criminals.

I want to let some light back in.

Rape. The word is so harsh. In Hindi, *balatkaar.* In Finnish, *raiskata.* In Indonesian, *memperkosa.* In Arabic, *aightisab.* In Slovenian, *posilstvo.* In Zulu, *ukudlwengula.* The English word "rape" probably comes from the Latin *rapere*—to snatch, to carry off. For the last seven hundred years, it's meant "to take by force." In Roman law, abducting a woman, whether or not you forced sex on her, was called "raptus." Which sounds horribly, misleadingly, like "rapture." Then again, the Oxford English Dictionary drily informs me that it comes from the word *rapa*, which means turnip. Even the definition is confusing.

I think about random examples from my own life—a male friend on a Nicaraguan beach with a woman friend, enjoying the night until someone beat him unconscious and raped her; a woman friend on another beach, in Greece, enjoying the day until a group of "cops" raped her; another woman really excited about a romantic evening with her new boyfriend until he grabbed her and forced himself on her. How have we managed to evolve as a species that is riddled with rape? When did we give ourselves permission to become this way? Sometimes I wonder if we consider bad table manners a worse breach of protocol than forcing a random object up a personal orifice.

I will be interested to see which shelves this book ends up on in bookstores. Essays? Not really. Sociology? Not learned or academic enough. Psychology? No, too opinionated. Research? Not comprehensive enough. Memoir? I hope not. It's easy to say what this book isn't, because it doesn't neatly fit into any genre. This is just what I want, because in this space lies my freedom. I can do whatever I want, and I have. I can roam around the world and the internet, stopping where I want, chatting with whoever takes my fancy, and drawing my own conclusions—or not. I am very willing to take shameless advantage of my street cred as a rape survivor to generalize and opine, but I speak only for myself, not for anybody else.

So what is this book? It's about what we talk about, but also what we *don't* talk about. We don't talk enough about aggravating phobias. We don't talk enough about rebuilding trust. We don't talk enough about joy and rage and how to fit both into our lives.

I began college weeks after being raped. I showed up at my freshman dorm still healing from physical injuries—a bump on my head and a bandage on my ankle. The ankle bandage wasn't because of anything the rapists did. A few days after the rape, I was at the beach, so happy to be alive that I took a running leap off the front steps of the house and twisted my ankle. In college, I threw myself into the feminist movement like a drunken sailor on shore leave—these were my people, this was my place! And it still is. When you're seventeen, with a bump on your head from almost dying and a bandaged foot from the rapture of living, clichés come easily. I joined marches and yelled, "Yes means yes! No means no!" Later, running in-service training sessions for police officers and doctors, I held forth on how rape has nothing to do with sex.

Now I realize that, well, sometimes yes doesn't mean yes; and sometimes rape *does* have to do with sex.

Much has changed in how we talk about rape. In the last few years, people in India have come a long way in talking about it in everyday conversation. In my household, rape is just another topic. If we can expose our children to talk of genocide, racism, bikini waxing, and the inevitable melting of the planet, why should we leave out sexual abuse?

Happily, the global conversation on this issue is deepening too: the #MeToo campaign has shone a startling spotlight on sexual harassment. This is all happening while the US has a robust champion of sexual abuse for its president.[1] It's particularly unsettling in contrast to the last occupant of the White House, a dignified, feminist man who believed in evolution—of the species, of ideas and attitudes. It's all very interesting, and confusing.

We must notice who is part of the conversation, and who is not. The #MeToo campaign is global, yes, but what is "global"? Let's not forget that the man who brings buffalo milk to my family home in rural Maharashtra, or the King of Swaziland's latest virgin wife, may not be on social media. Let's not forget that, if you're a trans person, your chances of being sexually assaulted are fifty-fifty[2]—but your chances of finding understanding and support, or justice, are far lower.

In this book, I will contradict myself. Rape is always a catastrophe. Rape is not always a catastrophe. Rape is like any other crime. Rape is not like any other crime. It's all true. Except for the foundational belief that rape is a *crime*, with a *criminal* and a *victim*, I will not take anything else for granted.

Rape drains the light. I want to let some light back in. I don't have answers, but I hope to at least illuminate some of the questions and assumptions we all carry around with us. We must talk about rape, and we must talk about *how* we talk about rape.

2

Who am I to talk?

She died from effrontery.

—Verlyn Klinkenborg, *The Rural Life*,
about an annoying mosquito

In 1980, I was seventeen, and had recently moved to the US with my family. I had just graduated from high school, and was spending the summer before college in my family home in Bombay with my father and grandmother, while my mother and brother were in the US. One evening, I was out with a male friend. We were accosted by four armed men, who forced us up a mountain, raped me, wounded us both, threatened to castrate my friend, almost killed us, but changed their minds after we made various promises, and released us hours later.

That's a pithy description of a long and gruesome night, but it really covers all the essentials. What happened later is far more interesting.

A few days after this, the local paper admiringly reported another story of abduction. A married couple was going home at night on their scooter. Some men stopped them on the road, and took the woman away. Her husband drove home without telling anyone. The next morning, she came home, went into the kitchen, poured kerosene on herself, lit a match, and went up in flames. According to the article, her husband didn't intervene.

My father and I both read the article. I think that was the moment it hit me that we must be a very odd family, because we simply couldn't understand it. Why didn't the man report the abduction? Why did the woman kill herself? Why did her suicide make her the hero of this story? Were we living in the same society?

I must be missing the Shame Gene that other Indian women are born with, because, for all the guilt, horror, trauma and confusion that followed my rape, it never occurred to me that I had anything to be ashamed of. Luckily for me, it didn't occur to my parents either.

Three years later, back in the States, I won a grant to do my undergraduate thesis on rape in India, and blithely showed up again, expecting rape victims around every corner to tell me all about it. It didn't quite happen that way.

I did find a group of women, including the fabulous Sonal Shukla and Flavia Agnes, two pioneers of the 1980s women's movement in India, who swept me along to Delhi, to the first national avowedly feminist gathering of Indian women. This blew my untutored mind and I went back to Bombay dangerously charged up. I don't know what sent me over the edge—all the people who kept saying rape didn't exist for "people like us," the upper classes; a dirty old man who heard what I was studying and decided it meant he could grope me; or just the growing conviction that I couldn't possibly be the only one, could I? Could I?

My new-found feminist friends stoked my indignation and encouraged me to write my story. I did. I went to the post office with the boy who was with me during the rape, and sent it off to a magazine in Delhi with a photograph.

There was no internet in those days, and so, rightly at the time, I thought that if *Manushi*, the women's magazine I had picked—the only publication of its kind in India in those days—did print it, it would appear and disappear quickly. Little did I know.

It did appear, and created a minor stir in India. Nobody had ever come out and talked about being raped before. And then the next issue was released, life went on, and thirty years passed. I never fully left the subject, while I went on living my life, writing books, doing odd jobs, traveling, becoming a mother. Even when it stopped being quite so personal, it was an intellectual challenge to grapple with sexual violence. I wrote my undergraduate thesis on rape. I wrote my graduate thesis on rape. For my first job out of college I was hired by a group of thirty-five fierce volunteers to run a rape crisis center in Cambridge, Massachusetts. I counseled survivors, raised funds, trained doctors and police officers and teachers, and learned a whole lot of useful lessons. Later, through many jobs and moves and relationships, I often returned to gender-based violence, increasingly out of fascination and passion rather than because of how it had affected me personally. I took pains to separate myself from the past—not because I was ashamed, but because other things took over and I didn't want to be boxed in by one thing. It all worked out well; life was good and full of love.

Then, on December 16th, 2012, Jyoti Singh, a young physiotherapy student in New Delhi, went out for an evening with a male friend. She was gang-raped on a bus, and left with grievous injuries. She died a few days later, and the country went into an uproar. The story electrified the country, and the world. It set off storms of protest in India, and exposed some truly horrendous aspects of our culture, and rape culture in general.

One protester's sign said, *Don't tell your daughter not to go out. Tell your son to behave properly.*

Another sign said, *Chop their raping tools.*

The Indian president's son, an MP himself, said, "Women who are participating in candle-light vigils and those who are protesting have no connection with ground reality. These pretty ladies coming out to protest are highly dented and painted."[3]

On film, one of the rapists said that only about twenty percent of girls are "good." If they go out at night with boys, they are asking for trouble. If they don't want to be killed, they should just lie back and submit. He and his friends were teaching Jyoti a lesson, he said, and her death was an accident.

(There must be a manual for rapists somewhere. That is exactly what the men who raped me said—that they were teaching me a lesson for my own good.)

One of the rapists' lawyers explained helpfully in the same film (*India's Daughter* by Leslee Udwin) that women are like flowers and men are like thorns. "If you put that flower in a gutter, it is spoilt. If you put that flower in a temple, it will be worshipped." Later he compared women to diamonds and men to dogs. I couldn't keep track of the metaphors after that.

Suddenly rape was trending. It was all over the news, part of every conversation, the topic of the moment.

Through all of this, I said nothing. I was horrified at the tragic story of Jyoti Singh's murder, heartened to see the crime getting so much attention, and relieved that I had nothing to do with any of it because I had done my bit three decades ago, and now other people were fighting the good fight.

Then, a couple of weeks later, on New Year's Day, I was on a train from Boston to New York with my family when I got an email from a friend in Delhi. "This is doing the rounds on Facebook." I clicked on the link and was transfixed to see my teenage face on my phone screen. Not being on social media, I had had no clue that somebody had dug out the old *Manushi* article, photo and all, and posted it. It instantly went viral. I was still the Only Living Rape Victim of India.

And then all hell broke loose. Rape is a lot about loss of control, and this was a very familiar feeling. I had spent thirty years getting past this, and it was back with no warning. My story was all over Facebook and Twitter and all the other platforms I didn't even know how to use. Relatives and friends who had no idea that this was part of my history were finding it on their phones and computers. Indian TV stations called and asked for interviews. The Western media, eager to capitalize on the buzzy news story of the world's new Rape Hot Spot, but with no actual victims to talk to, asked me for interviews. I just sat there, shocked, wondering when my eleven-year-old was going to ask about all the phone calls.

I said no to everyone, but over the next few days of mayhem I became increasingly confused. Should I respond? Should I let it die down? Was it my duty to speak? Who cared what I had to say, anyway? I didn't want to upset my mother by prolonging the attention. I didn't want the rape to define my life. But I didn't want my slightly overwrought manifesto of so long ago to be my last word on the subject, either. Should I say something?

My spouse sensibly said, "First decide if you have something to say." It sounds obvious, but I had been so busy spinning my wheels that I hadn't actually considered that. I thought back to what I had written in *Manushi*—the defiant cry of a young girl who refused to be ashamed. Then I thought of who I was now—a mother, a survivor, a writer. I remembered being on that mountain being raped, and bearing it all by dissociating and writing a news story in my head. Well, here was my chance to actually do it.

The piece I wrote was a distillation of many of the ideas in this book—the idea that rape doesn't have to define you, that it doesn't have to reflect on your family, that it is terrible but survivable, that you can go on to have a joyous life, and that four men on a mountainside don't have to own you forever. The *New York Times* ran it,[4] and I went live on their web channel to talk about it. The editors let me say most of what I wanted, although, to my abiding regret, they changed "I reject the notion that men's brains are in their balls" to "I reject the notion that men's brains are in their genitals." ("Balls" is just so much more evocative.)

Then all hell broke loose—again. I had put *myself* out there, this time, and so I had no right to whine, but I was still blindsided by the comprehensive panic that engulfed me when I woke up that morning and realized the paper was on my doorstep and on my computer, along with millions of other doorsteps and computers. I cowered under the covers at five-thirty a.m. and burst into tears. "I've changed my mind!" I wailed. "I don't want to do it." (I did the same thing when I was eight months pregnant—as usual, safely too late to change course.) Suddenly, "putting myself out there" seemed like an abysmally stupid idea. I didn't know what image they would use to illustrate the piece. They hadn't told me the title. I didn't want to know. I had to know.

My brother called at six a.m. "It's here!"

"Oh, my God. What's the title? Is it *Vagina Vagina Vagina Vagina Vagina*?"

It wasn't, and the image, though rather morose, wasn't offensive either. But it was all over most of the editorial page. My boss emailed me that he was on the subway and the guy next to him was reading it. A random guy in the sandwich shop said, "I know you!" Journalists called again. Friends, colleagues, and total strangers flooded me with emails and calls. My website got three million hits in one month.

To the journalists I said I was done; but I saved the emails, and replied to almost all of them. Very few were nasty, and some of the nasty comments were too funny to sting. I particularly cherished the man who thought I had made up the story to sell my novels. That would have required a lot of cunning and foresight, since the rape happened long before I wrote any fiction, but I appreciated the confidence in my marketing ability. Then there were many emails entitled "Hats Off!" and even one with "Heads Off!" People wrote from India, the US, Denmark, Australia, Saudi Arabia, the UK, Canada … Women wrote saying they had been raped and never told anyone; men wrote expressing horror and helplessness; a neighbor from India wrote to tell me I was "one helluva tough cookie indeed"; friends wrote to say they were weeping. It was all very interesting. Some of it was terribly sad. Imagine the loneliness of someone who is being raped by someone close to her, and has to write to a total stranger because she has never had anyone else to share her burden or ease her pain. When I clicked on an email, I had no idea whether it would make me grin ("You make it sound so dramatic, there is no reason for that") or cry ("I'm tired of feeling helpless. Tired of getting up in the middle of the night to terrifying nightmares of me being abused, and people watching, and me helpless").

It was odd, "outing" myself this way, because I was suddenly getting all this sympathy and support, which was lovely, except that I didn't need any of it. I was three decades past needing it. People who read it were shocked and upset that I had been through this, but I had finished being shocked and upset long ago. The story wasn't news to me. So I was in the strange position of comforting the people who wanted to offer me comfort.

If you're a survivor yourself and reading this, you know that when I write "I had finished being shocked and upset long ago" I don't mean it's done and dusted and put away and now I'm finished with the rape. I remember a male friend to whom I talked less than a year after it happened. "Do you think I'm thinking about it for too long?" I wanted to know. "I still feel scared and upset; do you think I'm making too big a deal out of it?" "Yes," he said, "you are. You should be over it by now." That shut me up for quite a while.

It took me a long time to see how clueless he was. You don't "get over it" so easily. It doesn't work like that. Rape is no different from any other trauma in that way—you can't make it unhappen. No matter how much you heal, you can never be *unraped*, any more than you can be undead. I mean that it is one of the patchwork of events that have made me the person I am. Sometimes it's upsetting; usually it's just there. I have made my peace with it—mostly.

I also felt a bit sheepish about getting so much attention. My novels never created a stir like this—now *that* would be a dream come true. Was I just cashing in on a sensational story to make waves?

Of course, the *New York Times* piece only finished what the reborn *Manushi* piece had already started—put me front and center as the Rape Victim. I was back to square one, and I've spent the last couple of years working hard once again to make sure that that is not what defines me. I wrote a newspaper column about many things that have nothing to do with rape—gardens, bicycles, architecture, education ...

So why on earth am I back, writing about it again? The fact is, even if it doesn't define me, it fascinates me. Now, more than ever before, people are writing and talking about rape. In the past couple of years quite a few brave people all over the world have spoken out about their own experiences of being raped. Sexual abuse is all over the Western media. I'm an odd sort of skeptical observer to it all: a brown bisexual middle-aged atheist Muslim survivor immigrant writer without a Shame Gene. Those are my qualifications.

Unlike Verlyn Klinkenborg's mosquito, who didn't know when to quit, I didn't die. I told the men who raped me that I would keep their secret. I made up a whole scenario about meeting them again if they let me go. I told them I had a disease. I told them that they were better than this. I told them about my grandmother. I tried every crazy argument I could think of to change their minds about committing murder. I talked non-stop. I talked my way out of oblivion. And I'm still talking.

3

Shut up or die, crazy bitch

I don't know why I am writing this email but I want to be free from the burden I am carrying inside my heart ... living through this nightmare seems almost impossible to me ... I have also tried to kill myself ... I don't know what to do with my life ahead.

—email, 2013

The first person I spoke to was my sister. She refused to believe me. He had raped me. I was bleeding and pregnant. He took my keys so I couldn't go to the hospital. I called my sister. She drove me to the hospital and I told her on the way. She said, "Khabardar,[5] if you tell anyone ... " She said I was a liar.

—Angie, raped and beaten by her husband
for years before leaving him

I TOLD MY story. Others don't, for so many reasons.

"Every morning I would wake up to him doing something." Rida was three or four. Her father was in the Army, and the family constantly moved between postings. In a small Maharashtra town, corporals were assigned to work in their houses as orderlies—glorified servants. "He" was one of these men.

It happened for months, maybe longer, she's not sure how long. "My pyjamas would be off and he would be on top of me. I remember fearing what my mornings would be like when I woke up. I would always try running away from him when I woke up."

She didn't tell anyone. "Some things you don't talk about. I recognized this very early on… One day I woke up and saw his full erection. He was a huge, bulky man. I kicked him very hard. It stopped after that."

She didn't have the words to tell anyone, and, looking back now, she thinks she probably understood that she would be blamed. "I was a tomboy. I was very friendly with everyone, no matter what class they were. I had no inhibitions. I was very comfortable with the household help. My parents didn't appreciate that. My family was quite conservative. Maybe subconsciously I felt they would blame me.

"We learned lessons like, 'Don't be found lying down by a man.'"

The first time she told anyone, she was seventeen years old and in college. Something happened then and she was with a group of friends talking about the incident. "*Every* girl had a story. More than one. I told them what had happened to me. I cried then. It was amazing. It was cathartic. I finally had a way to make sense of it. I felt like a weight actually lifted off me."

Some years later, she took a class where the students were given an assignment that involved writing to someone close to them and disclosing a secret. She wrote to her sister, telling her about the abuse. Then she called her sister to warn her that the letter about to arrive was very serious and to try not to be too shocked. Her sister read the letter and called immediately to say that the same man had done the same thing to her. They had grown up together, each alone with the same secret.

What happens when you keep such a big secret? What happens to you, and what does your silence mean for the people around you and your community?

It took Angie ten years to leave her husband, ten years in which she had nobody to confide in. "Some women have scars on them they can show. My scars are inside me," she told me. Manassah, a male survivor, spent many years feeling totally alone. When he finally met another man who had been raped, "It was awesome!"

Cheryl grew up in a small Midwestern city in the US. She was raped in high school by the most popular boy in class. Talking to me, she remembered how alone she felt. "I lived with it very quietly, very stressed out. I was already an anxious kid and this sent me over the edge. I was in classes with him. I started dressing differently, wearing baggy clothes and black. I wrote him a note—*Why did you do this?*—and he wrote back, *Leave me the hell alone, stop lying about me.*"

Why do we keep quiet? The easy answer is shame, and often that is the reason. We think it's our fault for being available or vulnerable or clueless. All over the world, we blame ourselves, quite unable to take on board that another human being committed the crime. It's easier to feel ashamed than to accept that someone violated us in the most viciously intimate way and we couldn't do anything about it.

Cheryl started telling me her story in a very familiar self-deprecating way: "The most popular guy in school asked me to help him with his homework. And I fell for it like a dumbass."

Heather was gang-raped. She told me why she avoided talking about it: "It was an issue of embarrassment, of disgust. My number one goal was to feel clean and forget what had happened. For me I think it was just, Okay, that's done. Clean yourself up and move on."

The men who raped me had a very sharp weapon, and every intention of using it on my friend and me. We lived because I promised them that I wouldn't talk, in exchange for not being murdered. They had no hesitation in believing me. They clearly knew Indian society better than I did.

Taboos are as varied as societies. In the townships of Port Elizabeth, South Africa, people do talk about rape. Busisiwe Mrasi is twenty-three. She has a huge white smile (and a perfect gap in her front teeth—to let the light in) and told me her story of being raped at nine. She's dealt with many challenges. She contracted HIV from the rapist. Her mother was an alcoholic and her father suffered from debilitating asthma. She lived alone for a while and went to school. Now she has a three-year-old son, and they both get solid health and education support through Ubuntu Pathways, which is how I connected with her. I asked Busisiwe if she talks about being assaulted. Absolutely, she said. "I tell people that I was raped, and living with HIV. I hear about other people, and I have that heart for them."

Nomawethu Siswana from Ubuntu says this is quite normal. People in the townships do talk openly about rape—as long as it is rape by a stranger. "It's secretive when a family member is the perpetrator."

If I felt fraught telling people that I was attacked at knifepoint by a bunch of strangers, I can't imagine how difficult it must be to talk about incest or rape within marriage or by an acquaintance, both of which are more common. In India, rape in close communities is actually one of the justifications for child marriage. Better for the girl to go to her in-laws while she's still a virgin, and get legally raped, before an uncle or neighbor gets to her.

Sanjana was molested by a family friend when she was nine years old. She didn't tell because she was sure it was her fault. "I loved the attention I got from him," she told me. He was a teenager, about eighteen. "We were friends," she explained. "I was just getting aware of my own sexuality and I wanted to explore. So when he raped me, I thought it was my fault. How could I tell anyone? My biggest fear was that my mother would find the blood in my panties!"

A South Asian woman wrote to me: "I was abused as a child by a relative. My father never believed me, and I didn't have the guts to tell my mother. I was confused and ashamed of what had happened. The sight of that man pricks and tears up my soul."

In the US, seven out of ten rapes are committed by someone the victim knows.[6] This increases both the self-blame and the cost of telling.

But there's more than just shame.

Telling doesn't always come with a reward: comfort, closure, justice. Sometimes, women tell but everyone acts as if they said nothing at all. One woman emailed me: "I told my parents about it and they did nothing. Absolutely nothing. I felt so betrayed. Everyone in my family knew but still he was there at each and every family function. He even works at my uncle's shop."

Sometimes, telling can cost you precious relationships. One grandmother holds your hand; the other gives you a death glare.

Sometimes you tell and you have to comfort the other person.

Sometimes you tell and the other person says something appalling. The day after I was raped, a friend, trying to cheer me up, said, "Wow, you were with four guys!"

And it isn't just relationships at the time; this goes on forever. Given how much baggage we all carry around about sexual violence, there's a perfectly justifiable reluctance to be open about having been raped. I told a potential boyfriend in grad school what happened to me, and that was the end of any chance of us getting close. He gazed at me with horror, as if I were a precious porcelain figurine that had been damaged by the big bad world, which it was *his* job to protect—which he proceeded to do by following me adoringly around campus until I got so creeped-out I had to be brutally rejecting. Who needs that?

Sometimes telling is just a huge commitment of time, energy and emotion. Telling is difficult because, while you can control whom you tell (unless someone posts your thirty-year-old rant on Facebook), you can't control their response. You get what you get. So, when you've just been violated so comprehensively, of course it makes sense to hold your pain close where nobody can make it worse.

As Heather told me more and more details of her gang-rape and its aftermath, I heard something very familiar in her voice. I know it well, because I have it myself: a way of telling the story in a smooth arc, matter-of-factly, with intonation but no real emotion. It's what we do to keep it slightly at arm's length, and it's a great coping mechanism. It is also rather curative—the more often we tell it, the more manageable it gets, because no matter how many details we share, we leave out the unbearable ones that nobody wants to hear. Finally we are left with a sanitized version, with the requisite sprinkling of horror, but nothing to make you too uncomfortable. And we are always making sure not to give you more than you can handle. We are protecting you.

Today, with women (mostly women with some privilege and safety) speaking out about abuse and rape and naming their abusers, it's hard to imagine the world I grew up in, when I could not imagine what the face of another rape victim would look like. But it's still a big deal. It's going to be a long time until rape is so stigma-free that there's no penalty for speaking out as a survivor. Sometimes that penalty is to be pigeonholed, somehow diminished.

In 2014, actor and writer Kalki Koechlin went to an event to highlight child sexual abuse. Chatting to someone at the event who praised her for attending and supporting the issue, she said something along the lines of "It's universal—it's happened to every woman, including me."

"I really didn't think it was a big deal to say it," she told me. "I was just making the point that it happens to everyone." She didn't give it a second thought.

"I woke up the next morning, and the whole world descended." People she knew, people she didn't know, media, family. They all wanted to know who it was. They all wanted to know what happened. It made the headlines; it made the TV news. She didn't answer any questions until some time had passed and she could talk about the topic more generally: "What happened isn't interesting." Kalki rapidly got tired of every interview, every conversation turning to this one topic. "I just deflect," she says. It's not because she is ashamed of her history—it's just that she doesn't want to be defined by this one thing.

I understand perfectly. It's quite a balancing act—you don't want to have a secret you can't share, but you equally don't want this one thing that happened to you to be the biggest thing on everyone's mind when they think of you. I hope being a rape survivor isn't the most interesting thing about me or anyone else. In the grand scheme, what happens *afterwards* is more important. Is Malala Yousafzai interesting solely because she was shot in the head by the Taliban? That is noteworthy, of course, but by now she is interesting because of what she has done with her life after that.

Telling may also rebound on the survivor. Imagine marshalling all your resolve to speak up, only to find that nobody believes you. I have to roll my eyes at all the overwrought fear of false accusations expressed by the current pack of US Department of Education hellhounds in charge of legislating campus procedures. Of course accused abusers should get due process—I love and respect many men, and if one of them were accused I would want him to get a fair hearing. But look around, people. Just look around. Where in the world is it pleasant to report a rape? I find it very hard to believe that droves of girls and women are rushing to say they've been assaulted when they haven't. Women still don't generally have an easy time reporting sexual assault. In fact, the opposite is too often true. Ask all the women who've had to eat their words.

I know what happened to me. The police didn't believe us, despite our visible wounds, and the doctor was too embarrassed to even examine me properly. If I ever feel crazy and delusional, I just have to pick up the phone and call the guy who was with me, who witnessed it all. Thank goodness for that. But if you look in the dusty ledgers of the local police station you will find a report, signed by me, stating that nothing happened that night. I remember sitting and writing it out by hand. That was the only way I could prevent the police from detaining me for "protection." If I had insisted on the truth, and on filing charges, I would have been locked up in a detention home. I would not have been allowed to leave the country, go back to the US to my mother, and begin college. So—I lied. But not about being raped. I lied about *not* being raped.

Do women ever lie about being raped? I'm sure some do. But false allegations are extremely rare.[7] Women can be psychopaths, too, and liars and opportunists. But anyone who thinks lying about rape is the default for the *victims* is delusional.

As if all these reasons for not telling were not enough, there is another false idea doing the rounds. Does telling make you a weak and whining victim?

It's an astounding, insidious motif all over the world—if you can't take it on the chin (or in the vagina) and get over it quietly, you're a wimp. Plenty of women have adopted this ridiculous mantra—the refrain of which goes something like this. If you complain about anything less than a full-on penetrative rape where your life was in danger, you're undoing all the work women have done to become powerful. You're giving up your agency and playing into stereotypes of weak, passive women. If you couldn't say no then, you have no right to speak now.

This is so wrong. The opposite is true. The minute you speak, the moment you write your own narrative, the *second* you open your mouth, you are no longer just a victim. You are taking back some control. It is the opposite of victimhood.

Anyone who thinks it's not brave to speak out hasn't faced disbelief, derision, or that most unsavoury of all responses—titillation. The friend who joshed me about being with four guys wasn't really titillated; she was just uncomfortable and blurted out the most inappropriate thing. I've done this too often myself to hold it against her. But for some people there is a level of titillation in rape stories. I suppose it's inevitable, given the act itself, but it's still gross. There's nothing erotic about someone slamming into your body like a truck, and nothing positive to be gained from seeing that slightly turned-on look in someone else's eyes when you tell him or her. I know it's kept me from speaking up sometimes, as I'm sure it has other people.

In Shakespeare's *Titus Andronicus*, Lavinia is raped and has her tongue cut out. Telling has a high price. But so does not telling. Not telling means you don't get physical or psychological help. You don't get tested for pregnancy or HIV. You don't get therapy. You don't get to sit in the sun with your best friend and have a good cry. It takes effort to keep a secret.[8] Sometimes remembering is too difficult and you bury it, but that doesn't necessarily work. "You forget," says a wise man (whom I married), "until forgetting is more difficult than remembering."

And that's just the price survivors pay. Keeping quiet about rape has a whole other toxic effect: it lets abusers off the hook. I want to be very clear that it is never a victim's obligation to speak up, or report, or do anything but survive. Her first responsibility is getting through it. But we are all culpable in the silence around rape, a "vast international conspiracy" if ever there was one.

Larry Nassar benefited from exactly this kind of conspiracy. A sports doctor for US Olympic-level gymnasts, he sexually abused hundreds of girls for years before he was stopped. Many of his victims did speak out long before he was finally arrested—it was the grown-ups in charge who kept their eyes and mouths shut. It was an epic, if not atypical, systemic betrayal.

"When it comes to silencing women," classicist Mary Beard has written, "Western culture has had thousands of years of practice."[9] So have other cultures.

Silence is powerful. But not as powerful as words. Look at the Harvey Weinstein scandal and the barrage of revelations that followed, about sexual abuse in a variety of arenas. Weinstein, a Hollywood mogul, has been accused, arrested and indicted for sexually abusing woman after woman for years.[10] His victims stayed mostly silent, or if they spoke out, it was only to their closest people. Then, in October 2017, the story burst wide open with a *New York Times* article about Weinstein's predatory behavior, which apparently had been an open secret in Hollywood. Star after star said she had been harassed, or worse, by him. Gwyneth Paltrow, Angelina Jolie, Rosanna Arquette, Ashley Judd, Asia Argento, Rose McGowan … the stories were revolting. The response, for the most part, was heartening. Others in the industry lavished support on the women who spoke out. Those who didn't were a distinct but vocal minority.

Words turned out to be more powerful than Harvey Weinstein's grip on the industry, and certainly more powerful than his dick, which way too many people have seen. Words are the enemy of impunity. They can create real change.

The Democratic Republic of Congo is dismally called "the Rape Capital of the World."[11] Whether or not that's true, it's certainly a strong contender for Impunity Capital of the World. In 2008, the UN officially designated rape a weapon of war (sometimes it takes the guys a few centuries to catch up semantically) and the DRC, where rape during armed conflict is so common that in Bukavu there is a hospital devoted to treating rape-related injuries such as fistula,[12] rapists have historically tormented women, men and children with no repercussions. In 2015, Lauren Wolfe, director of Women Under Siege at the Women's Media Center in the US, reported on rapes by MP Frederic Batumike Rugimbanya and eleven other men. She kept writing about it. In 2016 she wrote a piece in *The Guardian*[13] that led to sixty-eight arrests. She kept writing until the DRC government stopped delaying and held a military trial. In December 2017, all twelve men who were tried were given multiple life sentences for crimes against humanity. Their crimes included raping and murdering nearly fifty girls, from infants to eighteen years old. Words did that. Words led to the first time that an army official in the DRC was convicted of rape.[14] Lauren Wolfe refused to shut up, and helped give voice to all the victims and families who talked to her. Witnesses refused to shut up, although they were in so much danger that they had to cover their entire bodies, use voice-altering boxes, and even testify behind walls. Words drilled a hole in impunity.

But words are also a luxury. It takes courage for anyone at all to speak up about sexual abuse in any form. For many, many women, speaking up is lethal. For every woman, it takes guts. An established, rich, white Hollywood star deserves kudos for speaking out. A maid in a Mumbai apartment who is counting on her salary to support her children has to think a lot harder about outing her employer if he comes into her room at night. And, for women in joint families in villages, speaking out about incest or rape can literally mean death.

And so they keep quiet, and so it continues.

One marital rape survivor who talked to me said it best: "If we don't put it out there, this conversation will always be muted."

4

Totally different, exactly the same

*There is another world inside this one
no words can describe it.*

—Rumi

EVERY NOW and then something happens and we all get excited. This is a game-changer! Things will never be the same! A turning-point, a watershed, the moment it all changed. Or didn't.

December 16th, 2012 was such a moment in India, with the gang-rape and murder of Jyoti Singh in New Delhi. She was a young woman who had come from her village to the big city, full of ambition. She was a physiotherapy intern, and one evening she went to the cinema with a male friend. An ordinary evening out, which ended with her being gang-raped, eviscerated, and fatally injured, followed by a national outpouring of frustration and rage when she died.

Rape and murder are perfectly commonplace. The sun rises, someone is raped, the sun sets, someone is killed, the sun rises again. But this one touched a national nerve, and, while rape and murder are still as predictable as sunrise and sunset, the conversation has indeed changed.

For one thing, there *is* a conversation. That in itself is radical. Now we have a country where we acknowledge rape, and, for better or worse, get to hear our leaders pontificate on the subject. Now my mother's driver and I can calmly discuss rape in the car while he takes me somewhere.

Thirty years ago, I could never have imagined this. Consider what happened when I was researching my undergraduate thesis in 1983. Still clueless about the level of denial despite what had happened to me, I showed up in India with lots of notepads and my trusty fountain pen, with visions of long, intense conversations with women and men representing all sections of society. It didn't work out that way. The only survivor I met was a five-year-old child in a Bombay slum whose family was working with a women's group to try to keep her safe after she'd been raped. I ended up interviewing one single rape victim for my thesis: me. The other people I wrote about were all lower-caste women whose experiences had made it into the news because the Indian left was willing to talk about rape as long as it was in the context of caste and class oppression. This was laudable, but incomplete. A middle-class woman raped by lower-class men; a girl raped by men in her own family—these didn't fit the narrative. Feminist groups were fighting the good fight and trying to foster a more nuanced discussion of sexual assault, but it wasn't easy.

Why was the Jyoti Singh case such a flashpoint, when numerous cases before hers weren't? The Mathura case of

1972 certainly didn't have the same public impact. Mathura, an adolescent tribal girl, was raped by two policemen. There were protests and some outrage, but the rapists were found not guilty. The judge said the circumstances didn't justify a verdict of rape as she was "habituated to sexual intercourse."[15] Mathura's story is significant nevertheless: it jump-started the anti-rape movement in India. It got women organizing and marching in the streets. It was the first time a rape verdict in India was challenged. The entire country wasn't engulfed the way it was after Jyoti Singh, but Mathura galvanized feminists into a lasting outrage.

I don't know why Jyoti Singh was different. One theory holds that she represented a new India, a country where a young rural woman can come to the city with a dream, pursue a degree, have friends and freedom, go out with a friend at night to see *Life of Pi*, and live to tell the tale. She represented something new and exciting and hopeful, and destroying that was the final indignity that brought long-simmering rage to the boil.

Whether or not that's the reason, it did happen. Thousands marched in the streets. Her rapists were sentenced. One was a minor and got three years; four were given the death penalty. One has already died in prison in suspicious circumstances. On the streets and in the media, the furore led to discussions at the highest legislative levels: just ten days after the crime, the central government appointed a judicial committee to look into the law regarding sexual assault. The committee had a thirty-day deadline.

The Justice Verma Committee had three members: Justice Jagdish Sharan Verma, a highly regarded chief justice; retired justice Leila Seth; and ex-solicitor general Gopal Subramaniam. They invited the Indian public to weigh in on rape and rape laws, and within days over seventy thousand people responded. Seventy thousand people!

The committee's report[16] is hot stuff. I don't agree with all of it, but when was the last time the Indian government supported the creation of a feminist manifesto? Aside from recommending judicial reform, police reforms, and other obvious steps, the report went further and recommended systemic changes to alter rape culture and protect women—for instance, registering all marriages instead of allowing people to choose simply a religious ceremony. It blamed the government as well as public apathy. It discussed the rampant sexism that breeds an atmosphere of impunity.

It was far from perfect, but it was still a marvellous achievement. The people—ordinary people, women's groups, experts—spoke, and they were heard. Experts were called in and provided riveting testimony. The report called out some of the most toxic examples of government response ("The victim is as guilty as her rapists … can one hand clap? I don't think so."). It condemned as "outrageous stains on a free India" the many ways in which Indian women are oppressed. It quoted African-American singer and civil rights activist Marian Anderson. It even quoted me, much to my childish glee. It passionately defended the concept of gender fluidity. It stated unequivocally that rape victims can go on to "proceed with life in a positive way." This might not sound like much, but remember this is a country where the belief that it's better to die than be raped runs deep—rape victims are called *zinda laash*: living corpses. It said that "it is all the more necessary that we snap the link between shame and honor, on the one hand, and the crime itself." It abhorred the fact that the Indian police have become "arbiters of honour." It found it "simply deplorable" that the police assume that they have the moral capacity to pronounce upon the rights and wrongs of the rape victim as well as the rapist. It discussed "nuances of consent" and the complexities of parsing out the dynamics of choice and power. It absolutely rejected the notion that husbands cannot rape their wives: "The fact that the accused and victim are married or in another intimate relationship may not be regarded as a mitigating factor justifying lower sentences for rape."

Hot stuff! The report also thoughtfully explored the pros and cons of using the term "sexual assault," which allows for a broader definition, and "rape," which "continues to bring with it a high degree of moral and social opprobrium." It recommended keeping both terms—"rape" for its extra shock value and gravitas, "sexual assault" for its breadth. It looked to other countries—South Africa, Canada—for enlightenment on policymaking. It addressed so-called "Eve-teasing," sexual harassment at work for all classes of women including domestic workers, trafficking, abuse at national borders. It made a distinction between trafficking and prostitution, which is more enlightened than many a Western feminist. It called for families and schools to reconstruct ideas of gender roles. It laid out an excellent analysis of what happens all too often to Indian boys to turn them into jackasses in adulthood. It humanely rejected the death penalty for rape (nobody listened—we now have this in certain cases). It rolled its figurative eyes at the idea of chemical castration as a solution. Instead, it called attention to problems such as the high percentage of criminals in elected office, the lack of facilities and training in medical and police facilities, and the rampant discrimination that sullies every nook and cranny of Indian life.

The report is inspiring, thoughtful, necessary. It's not easy reading. When I got to page 215 of the 656 pages, I had to put it aside for a while: it was delving into the horrifying treatment of children in juvenile homes. The world can be so foul, so malign. So ready with its ragged, glistening teeth to devour the most vulnerable.

This report would never have been written before the events of December 2012. It is an astonishing document marking a watershed moment. And yet.

And yet. I wonder how much real difference all the huffing and puffing has made. Has all this discussion and awareness prevented even one rape? The news is consistently full of child rape, gang-rape, viral filmed rape, rape, rape, rape.

Jyoti Singh's family is not satisfied that things have changed enough. (Although how could they be, really? What would need to happen to make them feel their daughter didn't die pointlessly? She *did* die pointlessly.) Indian women still feel unsafe. Reported rapes are up, true, but who really reports rape, and what happens afterwards? One study of reported rapes in Delhi found that forty percent of the rape complaints filed were actually by parents who had found out that their minor daughters were having consensual sex, and were turning to the courts to punish their children and their lovers.[17]

That's just another instance of rape being used as a tool for something else, and of the overwhelming complexity of the issue. On January 17th, 2018, the body of an eight-year-old girl was found in the jungles of Kathua in the Indian state of Jammu and Kashmir. She had been raped, strangled with her own scarf, and murdered by her rapists, who had bashed her head with a rock. Eight years old. In a scenario reminiscent of Jyoti Singh, India took to the streets. But this time there was another ugly element to an already staggeringly ugly situation—communalism. It turned out that the child's alleged attackers (including four police officers) were Hindu nationalists who had raped her as part of their campaign to frighten away her tribal Muslim community. And now, among the people protesting in the streets, there were those who were marching in support of the attackers. So we have sexism, caste, politics, power, all coming together to eliminate one small eight-year-old—a little girl who had named her horse Beautiful—from the world.

The Kathua rape had a clear political motivation, but, like all rape, it was more than one thing. If it had been just political, one of the men would not have asked the others to wait a few minutes before finishing her off so he could rape her one more time.

In the past, Indian police resisted opening rape cases. In my own case, they worked strenuously, and successfully, to prevent me from blotting their area's reputation by reporting a rape. Has that changed, with the new openness? Certainly, more cases are reported than ever before, but one thing stays the same: the victim remains the least important factor.

An administrator in a Mumbai orphanage for girls told me that in the last few years, since rape has become part of the national conversation, several children have been brought to the orphanage after being raped, usually by neighbors or relatives. These girls are not orphans. Their parents, eager for justice, filed First Information Reports (FIRs) with the police, and promptly lost all control of their daughters' fates. Police locked up the accused rapists, but also took the girls away from the parents. Now, the administrator told me, "The parents are crying—they want their children at home. The children are crying—they want to go home. As if being raped wasn't enough, they are being separated from their families. The police are putting pressure on them, and saying, if you don't testify, this man will go free. The children are going to have to speak in court."

This weird fervour to dramatically solve the problem—lock 'em up, string 'em up, rationality be damned—is a tempting fix. In the wake of the Kathua rape and murder, India quickly passed a law mandating the death sentence for child rape. In a culture where the justice system is so skewed, any sentence that final would be dangerous in any case. Besides that, compelling research shows that death sentences don't deter crime.[18] Besides *that*, capital punishment is just wrong. I deeply believe what I wrote in a newspaper column: "Hanging them high will diminish us all."[19]

The Verma report, like all the films and all the books (including, I hope, this one), and all the heated public and private discussion, matters. Without conversation and communication, we are doomed indeed.

Similarly, in the US and globally, the Harvey Weinstein revelations created a moment of catharsis and truth-telling. The #MeToo campaign made it impossible to ignore the scope of sexual harassment and rape, at the same time as we were treated to some unsavoury glimpses of rape culture. Think of the Republicans desperately hiding behind the Bible to justify a would-be Alabama senator's history of alleged sexual assault. He didn't win, and our expectations have become so low that we were actually surprised. We celebrated his loss, instead of taking it for granted that an alleged sex abuser would never be elected to national office. After all, we had all been watching men and women on the news talking about how much they supported him. And the election was a close one. Some voters accused his accusers of negative politics. I could practically smell the self-righteous breath of the woman who filled my screen with her stern face and spat, "Where have these ladies been for the past forty years? I'd like to see these ladies apologize."

One of the rape survivors who spoke to me for this book was adamant that she would not have agreed to talk if it weren't for #MeToo. "I'm so grateful for it," she said. "It gave me a voice." She wouldn't have had the courage to speak about her rape, and speaking about it is the start of working it out in her life. I know that, if I were seventeen right now, I would have a very different recovery process after being raped. I would not be nearly as alone.

The #MeToo movement is important, but it is not unique. Conversations that start in the US are always differently weighted. I went to a feminist discussion that included Jac sm Kee, women's rights program manager for the Malaysia-based Association for Progressive Communications. Jac said, "The internet is connected to geography. It's not just space, it's a specific space." She is right—while everyone can access the internet at least theoretically, the US dominates it in terms of content.

By way of example, she spoke of the Primavera Violeta (Violet Spring) in Mexico. Unless you're from Latin America, you probably haven't heard of it, and that's my point. In April 2016, two writers, one Colombian and one Mexican, put out a call on Twitter asking women to post about sexual harassment. Thousands spoke out, thousands marched in the streets, and gender-based violence became part of the national discourse. And yet, for many of us living north of that border, #MeToo was the first phenomenon of its kind.

This doesn't take away from the power of the movement in the US and across the globe. It's just worth remembering that #MeToo does not exist in a vacuum. It is part of something already happening in different places. It took many conversations, many editorial meetings, many classroom discussions, many social media posts, to create the moment when it all exploded, seemingly out of nowhere.

It definitely didn't spring out of nowhere. Although I've been following the movement, I didn't realize until I looked carefully that it didn't begin with one celebrity tweet in the fall of 2017. It began twenty years earlier in 1997, when a thirteen-year-old girl told Tarana Burke, a black woman, about being sexually abused. Burke was haunted by the story. Ten years later, she founded a non-profit organization to support sexual assault and harassment victims. She also founded a movement and named it MeToo. A woman of color, a non-celebrity, far from Hollywood, originally coined the now-familiar phrase.

In India, Mexico, the US, the world, these moments happen, rape or other forms of sexual violence become fodder for headlines and arguments and moments of reckoning, and then. Then, life continues, but maybe a little differently on both the personal and the global level. #MeToo won't end sexual harassment in either Hollywood or the corner shoe store, but I hope victims won't feel quite as alone. Or perpetrators quite as untouchable. Now, in many arenas, a woman who says she has been harassed, no matter what actually happens, will know that she isn't the only one. This is powerful. Similarly, I hope that a significant number of men who might not care about the ethics of abusing someone will hesitate because they do care about the possible repercussions.

It must be said, however, that, while very many people felt empowered by the national conversation to speak out and take charge of their own recovery, shining a spotlight doesn't always add to victims' comfort level. If you've been succeeding in burying something terrible that happened to you, it's very destabilizing to get reminders at every dinner party and every time you turn on the news. In the wake of #MeToo, rape crisis centers reported being extra-busy.[20] It's not easy being reminded about something you've tried hard to put behind you. Whether or not it's productive in the long run, it's terrifying to face something if you're not ready. Bringing things out into the open is ultimately good for all, but it can be terribly difficult for individual people if the timing isn't right, or if they lack the tools to cope. I know of one man, a sober alcoholic, who went into a tailspin when #MeToo gained momentum. He hadn't told his family about his childhood sexual abuse, and the sudden reminders everywhere were too much for him. He started drinking again, and has a long, hard road ahead.

I experienced something similar in college. Although I was open enough in talking about it, I really put my rape experience into a little mental box of things that just don't happen in the real world. It happened, but it was up on a faraway mountain in a faraway place, and now I was an undergraduate in beautiful Massachusetts. It was a different world, the same rules didn't apply and I was safe. Until March 6th, 1983, when Cheryl Araujo was gang-raped on a pool table in a bar in New Bedford, Massachusetts[21] (her story later became the subject of a film, *The Accused*, starring Jodie Foster). Suddenly rape was just sixty-four miles away, not 7,600. I read the newspapers and turned into a complete wimp. It was as if someone had let out all the air keeping me afloat and replaced it with terror. Thank goodness for good friends.

It had to happen. I believe it is ultimately positive to face things, however ugly. But I know how hard it can be when you don't get to choose when and how you face them. All the victims who hear the past icily whispering in their ears when rape comes to the forefront in the media deserve compassion.

And then, of course, since the media can be as fallible and gullible as the rest of us, much of what we read and hear is just plain wrong. Or distorted. Or subjective. Or just perpetuating old stereotypes.

So yes, we have defining moments, and they are very important. But they are never one-dimensional, they are always difficult, and they always exist in a context of messiness and confusion.

Defining moments shine a light on this or that group, this or that country, this or that event. The problem with spotlights is the surrounding darkness. In the US, for all the spilled ink, we don't have too many passionate Twitter debates about the fact that Native Americans are more than twice as likely to be raped or otherwise sexually assaulted as any other race.[22] In India, when I tried to talk about rape with my ageless tribal friend Mati, she laughed heartily at the idea that any justice could exist, anywhere. In New Zealand, Maori women are twice as likely to be sexually abused as children as women of other races.[23] In Australia, indigenous (Aboriginal and Torres Strait Islander) people endure higher rates of family violence, and are more likely to be sexually assaulted at university.[24] In the US, more than ninety percent of people with developmental disabilities are sexually assaulted.[25] It goes on. Most of the time, the rest of us aren't even conscious of the millions of people who don't share our language, media access and privilege, who won't read this book, and who won't wear pussy hats and march to have rights over their own bodies.

Jyoti Singh, the election of Donald Trump, #MeToo, the Kathua rape/murder, UK MPs calling for an end to bringing up rape victims' sexual histories in court… We've started talking about rape, and these big dramatic moments are merely highlights in the ongoing discourse. They are markers along a very long journey towards what scholar and lawyer Catherine MacKinnon calls "shifting gender hierarchy's tectonic plates."[26] Breakfast conversation, random tweets, stories in the Metro section—it is all part of the conversation, and it all matters. But the conversation doesn't include everyone, not yet. Let's keep talking.

5

Yes, no, maybe

Confucius, he say girl with skirt up, she run faster than man with trousers down, eh?

—Colin Dexter, *Last Bus to Woodstock*

Men are afraid women will laugh at them. Women are afraid men will kill them.

—attributed to Margaret Atwood

YES MEANS YES and no means no.

If it were that simple, this book would fit on an index card. But here we are, pondering the meaning of consent. It's both really easy and really difficult.

Blue Seat Studios created a charming little video, *Consent: It's Simple as Tea.*[27] It uses stick figures to illustrate why having sex is like a cup of tea. If you wouldn't force someone to drink tea, why would you force them to fuck? If someone said they wanted tea, and then changed their mind when you made it, would you pour it down their throat? And so on.

It's a nice tool for children. But sex isn't a cup of tea. If you don't really want a cup of tea, but you drink it because you're afraid you'll offend your host, that's good manners. If you don't really want sex, but you do it because you're afraid you'll offend your date (this happens all too often), that's not quite the same thing. It might not quite be rape, and then again, it might be—what are you afraid your date will do if you say no?

A friend of mine went to a brothel when he was a teenager. He had had only a few sexual experiences and wanted to expand his horizons. He went swaggering in and put his money down. A sweet and very young-looking girl took him into a little room. "We both sat on the bed," he told me, "and I didn't know what to do. She was just looking at me. So I said, 'Take your clothes off.' She said no."

"So then?" I asked.

"I didn't know what to do. Was I supposed to force her? She said no! I said okay. Then we lay down next to each other for a while, then the time was up and I left."

This makes perfect sense to me. Yes, he paid for sex. But, if she didn't want to take her clothes off, he had no right to rip them off. He could have asked for his money back, but he was correct not to force her. It's obvious to me, but plenty of people might think that, once he'd paid, she was his to do with as he pleased.

Being a sex worker doesn't mean you deserve to be raped. Neither does being a spouse. Again, your ability to consent depends on who you are, and where you are. In Canada, raping your wife is a crime (except if you come before Superior Court Justice Robert Smith, who ruled that a man who didn't *know* it was illegal to force intercourse on his wife was not guilty[28]). In India, Ghana, Jordan and numerous other places, once a woman is married to a man, she signs over the rights to her vagina (and the rest of her body) to her husband.[29] No consent? No problem. The law says marriage means full access, no questions asked.

In Kuwait, if you rape someone you're not married to, you can get out of trouble by marrying your victim.[30] Thankfully, governments across West Asia are realizing how inhuman these laws are. Getting married to re-brand a rape as an act of lovemaking looks more like state-sponsored sadism than criminal justice. And let's not fall into the common trap of vilifying only the Muslim world. In Italy, Article 544 of the Penal Code also allowed rape to be canceled by marriage. This goes to the heart of the true meaning of consent, and what you are actually consenting to. According to Article 544 (made famous in the 1960s by Franca Viola, a girl who refused to marry the man who kidnapped and raped her), sexual violence is a crime against morality, not against a human. This meant it could be fixed by marriage. Just think—you could erase all the bad juju caused by rape by simply going to church and having a *matrimonio riparatore* with your rapist. The law was finally abolished in 1981.

Now that heterosexual couples aren't the only ones allowed legally to marry in more and more places, it will be interesting to see how rape laws evolve. Will men be allowed to rape their husbands? Or will the power dynamics shift with the gender dynamics?

I had four men with weapons threatening to kill both me and someone I loved. They made him drop his pants, held a knife to him, and said they would castrate him and kill us both if I didn't stop fighting. So I did. I "let" them rape me. I "chose" rape over death. Some people might call that consent. Harvey Weinstein and various other Hollywood bigwigs allegedly threatened to shame women or ruin their careers if they didn't give in.[31] Does this mean the women gave consent? What about if one or both parties is drunk? Kim Fromme, a blackout expert, appears regularly in court as an expert witness to say it's possible to consent while blackout-drunk.[32] According to this point of view, you aren't competent to drive a car or operate machinery, but you're fully able to consent to sex.

It's all very confusing. Suddenly "yes means yes and no means no" starts to look very murky. There are just so many exceptions, in the laws and in our minds.

Vanessa Grigoriadis, author of *Blurred Lines: Rethinking Sex, Power, and Consent on Campus*, said in an interview:[33]

What we're really talking about is a new standard for consensual sex. That's the way we're talking about sexual assault now. I was always taught that rape is only about power, and not about sex. But no, not in this area. Not in the kind of sexual assaults we're talking about. We really have to talk about sex itself, and the way that post-adolescents are having it, and get into that conversation that nobody really wants to have in order to kind of make substantial changes here, because the programs that they're running for orientation really don't work ... Don't ever write a book about rape. That's my No. 1 tip.

Some US universities have instituted "affirmative consent" guidelines. That sounds great, but how many teenagers are going to sit down beforehand and discuss exactly what they're going to do, how they're going to do it, and precisely how willing they are? Sex doesn't always work that way, no matter what age you are. We can and must talk to our children about making sure they participate in consensual sex, but no amount of prescribed language can make up for basic mutual respect. Yes, ask, look for signals, keep your dick in your pants until you're really very very sure, but, in the end, you have to care. You have to care about another person's wishes and feelings.

And about their desires. Jaclyn Friedman, a sexual consent educator in Massachusetts, has the wisest words for this, capturing the real worth of parsing out consent: "Affirmative consent changes the morality at the core of sexual interactions." [34]

Let us consider, and hang our heads in shame about, the extremely low bar we set for "consent." Consent to what? A man having an orgasm and a woman letting him? A prisoner submitting to a guard to gain protection from further abuse? An old woman with dementia putting up no fight when the nursing home attendant gets handsy? That is such a poor standard. Sex is about pleasure and joy, for both (or however many are part of the action) willing participants. Let's aspire to this!

Female orgasms definitely don't play a major part in conversations around consent in India. In fact, "consent" often doesn't play a major part in conversations around sex, and certainly not when it comes to defining sexual violation. Madhumita Pandey, [35] a doctoral student at Anglia Ruskin University in the UK, has spent years talking to convicted rapists in Delhi's notorious Tihar Jail. She interviewed more than a hundred men. In the beginning she thought of them as monsters; by the end, she came to see them as human. They were poor, abused, battered by their circumstances, victims of caste, class and economic injustice. (Kindly note, though: girls living in poverty, and dealing with all these issues and misogyny, don't generally go out and rape to vent their frustrations.) They were just ordinary men with ordinary values, and no concept of consent. Most of them didn't even think of their crimes as rape. Granted, her research population was not typical—only the most disenfranchized men actually go to jail for committing rape in India. But plenty of men whose wealth and power insulate them from punishment share the same values.

Jaclyn Friedman writes:[36]

The basic principle at the heart of affirmative consent is simple: we're each responsible for making sure our sex partners are actually into whatever is happening between us. Since decent human beings only want to have sex with people who are into it, this shouldn't be a hard sell. But if you've been raised to think of sex as a battle of the sexes, or a business deal in which men "get some" and women either "give it up" or "save it" for marriage, it can still be a jarring idea, like suggesting to someone that there's something they could breathe other than air ...

In the absence of comprehensive, pleasure-based sex ed., we rely on media and other cultural institutions to model what sex should be like. Whether you turn to abstinence propagandists, mainstream pop culture, or free internet porn to fill in those gaps, you're likely to wind up with an incredibly narrow and bankrupt idea of how sex works, one that positions men as sexual actors, women as the (un)lucky recipients of men's desire, and communication of consent as lethal to both boners and romance ...

Teaching affirmative consent does something profound: it shifts the acceptable moral standard for sex, making it much clearer to everyone when someone is violating that standard ... Affirmative consent, when taught well, also removes heteronormative assumptions from sex ed. If we're each equally responsible to make sure our partner is enthusiastic about what's happening, gender stereotypes—such as that women are passive and men are aggressive— about sexuality begin to break down ...

Consent education does something else transformative: it tells girls that sex is supposed to be for them.

How do we teach our children, our partners, and ourselves, about consent? Consent is not even an issue in many, many situations. The men who raped me were going to rape me no matter what, and my only choice was whether to live or die. But most of us, as sexual beings, find ourselves in ambiguous situations. And for those of us curious about how we navigate those confusing currents of yes/no/ maybe, help is available from an interesting quarter: the BDSM community.

BDSM refers to Bondage & Discipline, Dominance & Submission, and Sadism & Masochism between consenting adults. Wait, don't run away! Remember, *consenting adults*.

"BDSM is a structured culture that exists for adult humans to play with and explore power dynamics in erotic ways," Tina Horn explained to me. "You can show you care by spanking someone really hard—if they want it."

Tina Horn hosts a podcast called *Why Are People Into That?!* She is a journalist, sex worker, sex educator, and pornographer. She worked as a dominatrix for many years in several US cities. While I have absolutely no desire to either spank or be spanked, I do think she makes a good point about respecting other people's wishes, about just listening. Even if you're not into leather and whips, there's something to be learnt from a subculture that values structure and negotiation. It's not particularly complicated: if you grow up thinking that your needs are paramount, you are less likely to pay attention to, or care, about your partner's feelings. BDSM actually mirrors some of the best features of affirmative consent: before getting down to the business of pleasure, check with your partner. Agree on what you're doing, how to signal that you want to stop, and how to pick up that signal. Sex is more fun when you're in it together. Being in tune with your partner(s) doesn't remove mystery; *au contraire*, it's an alluring joint adventure.

Tina insists that we would have a healthier society if BDSM were destigmatized. I think we would have a healthier sexual society if *sex* were destigmatized: if women stopped feeling bad about having desire, and men stopped feeling entitled. By "feeling entitled" I mean that consensual sex isn't like a train journey—buying a ticket doesn't mean you're entitled to ride to the end of the line. A lot of people, from rapists to parents to policymakers, don't seem to grasp this. In 2017, a California judge dismissed the charge against a twenty-year-old college student who was accused of raping a fellow student.[37] The judge cited videos showing the woman following the man out of a club, and letting him into her room. This, according to the judge, showed that she was the initiator.

So what? So what if she was the initiator? If she was drunk, or she changed her mind after they were in the room, or she changed her mind after they were both naked and the condom was already on—if she changed her mind at any point, and he didn't listen, that was the point at which she stopped consenting. There's no guaranteed ticket to the end of the line.

Sometimes the individual woman does say yes, but that doesn't make the encounter less abusive. When Sanjana told me about being raped as a child by an adolescent boy whom she hero-worshipped, she said she loved his attention, and wanted to explore her own budding sexuality. When he finally forced her to have intercourse, she was upset and reluctant, but, "You don't want to say no to a friend. I just wanted to be polite!" So he raped her. She didn't say no, she didn't say yes, she didn't want to do it, she was a child, and he was big and strong.

We talk about consent as if it all boils down to one person saying yes to one other person. And, while that is the ultimate frontier, I think a lot about institutional consent. It takes a whole intricate scaffolding for abuse to flourish. For instance, in India, mothers-in-law often wield immense power. In case after case of spousal murder, we learn that it is the mother-in-law who made the dowry demands, and the mother-in-law who poured the kerosene over the tormented wife and set her on fire. It's complicated to look at women's agency in a system of abuse, but we must.

The dowry system in India, homophobic laws in Africa and the Caribbean, the unbridled power of spiritual leaders from gurus to rabbis to imams to priests—there's a whole cast of enablers. And then it hardly matters what the individual woman says or doesn't say. The network of collusion and complicity in Hollywood that came jarringly to light during the #MeToo campaign is another example of institutional consent: you know you can get away with it because the whole system is set up to help you get away with it. This is a glittering example, because it involves movie stars and designer gowns, but it is no less real, menacing or horrifying for its victims. It is a rarefied example of a system built to support and condone abuse. A friend confided in me that she is having trouble feeling sorry for some of the famous actresses who are coming forward to talk about being abused by powerful men. "They made a choice to keep quiet," she said. "They went along with it, got what they wanted, and now they're talking."

"But why are you only thinking about *their* choices?" I wanted to know. "What about the choices the men made?"

So often we tend to talk about the victims and the ways they went along with, or took advantage of, or kept suspiciously quiet about, rape. They didn't leap up and stab the man and go running out clutching their clothes to their outraged bosoms, therefore they consented.

Saying "But she consented" is just one of the myriad ways we are so quick to blame the victim. Yes, we have choices. We choose between humiliation now or humiliation later, we choose between short skirts and long, we choose when to leave and when to stay. We choose when to say yes is just easier than saying no, at least in that moment. None of these choices equals consent.

On top of it all, we choose to blame each other—maybe out of misogyny, maybe simply out of fear—forgetting, as we do so, that there is someone else in the picture who also has a choice: a man, who can choose between decency and dominance.

6

What did you expect?

"What is it about me, that other people want to treat me this way?

—Audrey, Central Park, New York, 2017

AUDREY IS British, thirty years old, the happily married mother of a small son. She doesn't take her happiness for granted—she worked hard for it. Six years ago, she was raped by four men in Italy.

"I was twenty-four. I had been in Rome for a year. I was young, I had my first job; it was exciting. I was meeting lots of new people. I went out a lot. One night I met friends at a cool, rowdy nightclub. I had too much to drink. I can't remember details. It's all blurry: nightclub, colors, people.

"The next morning I woke up feeling sick. I was naked in a strange place. There was one person just looking at me, with disgust. I had an overpowering desire to leave. I asked him where we were and he told me the street address. I just wanted to get out of there.

"It was daylight. I was disorientated and unsettled. It was strange passing people on the street. I went home. It was Sunday morning. First I showered, then I slept for hours.

"I had bad feelings but I couldn't articulate them to myself. One of the friends from the night messaged me, and I messaged back, 'Men are such assholes,' but I didn't know why I said it.

"On Monday I met up with an acquaintance, who started talking about his friends who were boasting about what they had done to a girl. I realized it was me! I reacted and said they shouldn't have done that. He said, 'You were drunk in a nightclub; what did you expect?' I felt awful. I was very ashamed of drinking. I was embarrassed to think I might have been flirtatious with them. I was humiliated. What is it about me, that other people want to treat me this way?"

Audrey was so drunk that she didn't even remember leaving the nightclub, or who she was with. By Italian law, she was incapable of giving consent. But that didn't stop her from blaming herself. Why her? Why, of all the women in the bar, did they choose her?

Despite her feelings of guilt and responsibility, she took her assailants to court, after the police found them through her acquaintance. She had to wait almost a year for the final judgement. Despite plenty of loving support from her family and friends, "It was like a crushing weight that whole year. In Rome, I looked at the metro tracks and thought, I understand people who jump."

She met her assailants in court. "The feeling I got from them was *disprezzo*—disdain."

It's significant that the reason the case made it into the court system in the first place was because the rapists boasted about what they did to a friend. They were triumphant and proud that they had taken advantage of her vulnerability (she is quite sure they helped this along by drugging her), and they were certain both that this was something to show off about and that it carried no consequences for them. It's not unusual: rapists, so pleased with themselves that they simply must share the glory.

The case was dismissed. The judge said they were normal men, and therefore they couldn't be criminals. Audrey had been sexually active before that night, therefore she hadn't been raped. A friend to whom she explained this reasoning was as flabbergasted by it as I hope you are, dear reader. She said, "That makes no sense: if you had sex before, all it proves is that you know how to consent! You've had sex before, but you've never been raped before."

Audrey told me, "The judge said there was 'insufficient proof of lack of consent' therefore the case should be dismissed. He adopted the position held by the defense lawyer and initially expressed by the public prosecutor. Namely, they all made the inference that, because I went clubbing a lot at the time, and because I was not a virgin, it was reasonable to think I had consented, even though I said I was too intoxicated to do so and the men claimed to have been sober.

"In addition, there was this 'boys will be boys' notion floating around. These young men had no criminal records—sure, what they did wasn't nice, but did we really want to send them to jail? That would be a shame. Some of this wasn't explicit, but was evident in what the judge chose to emphasize in explaining the decision: why had I left the bar with the men to begin with? Also, I had not immediately gone to the police upon waking up in the strange apartment—if I had been raped, the thinking went, why didn't I fly out of there like a bat and report the crime? In reality, not much time elapsed. I went to the hospital as soon as I realized what had happened. The police came to me the next day. It was too late to test my blood alcohol level or for the presence of date rape drugs, unfortunately, but long enough for me to collect my thoughts and figure out that something had gone terribly wrong. I have always found this expectation that one instantly report the crime unfair, especially when, in my situation, I really had no idea what had happened, though I certainly felt awful and spent much of the next day between sleep and tears."

After time and therapy, Audrey has found a measure of peace. "I didn't erase it, but I reframed it," she explained. She no longer thinks she caused her rape, and she has created a full life for herself. "I didn't want these four assholes to control my life."

If you had your wallet stolen on a dark, deserted street, you might kick yourself for being out late, or having too much cash in it, or not looking over your shoulder, but you probably wouldn't feel you deserved to be robbed and beaten, and you would probably think of yourself as the victim, and the person who mugged you as the criminal. With sexual assault, that formula doesn't work.

A Montana lawyer, Lisa Kauffman, defended her client, who had allegedly raped a thirteen-year-old patient at a teenage addiction recovery center, by saying the girl was a "temptress."[38] Short skirts, make-up, driving a car, leaving your hijab at home. Being born female. We get the blame from all sides; of course we internalize it.

I know much of the confusion comes from sexist attitudes and cultural norms. But I think there is another aspect to the ease with which we blame ourselves for terrible events. It has to do with that familiar word: control. And if that's the case, then it's not necessarily completely pathological to blame yourself a bit. Maybe it's a coping mechanism.

Strong Island is a film about the murder of a young African-American man, William Ford Jr. The filmmaker, Yance Ford, is the victim's sibling. He made history in 2018 by being the first trans director to be nominated for an Oscar. In one section of the film, talking about how he blames himself, he puts an interesting spin on the guilt he carries around:[39]

> *The madness that is my brother's death, would drive me mad, if I weren't able to hold myself accountable for at least a small part of it. Because then … it sort of of … it grounds it somewhere. It puts it on the earth. As opposed to in the ether, or as opposed to in … in the unknown. Or in the anonymous. If I don't ground it, in some way, in myself, then it's everywhere, all the time. It's ubiquitous. And that's actually a greater, more damaging, heavier burden to live with, than to blame myself for not being a smarter nineteen-year-old when my brother called me and told me about this stupid fight that he had. Does that make sense?*

A giant light bulb went off in my head when I saw this clip. Maybe self-blame isn't always about self-hatred and internalized patriarchy. Maybe sometimes it's a convoluted way of making the whole thing less scary. The fact that this is delusional reasoning hardly matters—when you're seventeen, it's easier to think that it wouldn't have happened if you hadn't worn that shirt than that people might just hurt you because they feel like it and there isn't a damn thing you can do about it.

Of course, this doesn't justify *other people* blaming the victim. They have no excuse whatsoever and should all be smacked firmly on the head. But it does make me think just slightly more kindly of women I've told over the years, who have said things like, "Oh, I would never let that happen to me." In my more forgiving moments, I see this as self-protection rather than insensitive assishness, which, if it isn't a word, should be.

A woman walks into a hardware store. It sounds like the beginning of a joke, but it's actually the beginning of one of the videos [40] made by the "It's On Us" campaign to demonstrate just how cracked some of our justifications for rape are.

So, a woman walks into a hardware store. She sees a row of toilets for sale, sighs with relief, sits down on one, and starts to pee. The salesman goes up to her in horror and asks her to stop. "I can't just stop," she says. He threatens to call the cops. "Dude, what's your problem?" she says, peeing all the while. "I come in here with a biological urge that I can't be expected to control, you've got everything just out on display … and then you're shocked when I come in here and let nature run its course? Really?" She finishes and stalks out, with one parting shot: "Next time, get your signals straight."

It's really funny when it's a woman peeing in a display toilet. Not so funny when you think of the millions of men in the world who justify rape like this, and even less funny when you think of the ways in which we blame victims, and they blame themselves.

When Alexa told her mother that her ex-boyfriend burst into her dorm room, threw her on the bed and raped her, her mother said, "What did you think was going to happen?"

When Audrey told her acquaintance that she was the woman his friends had taken home from a nightclub and raped, he said, "What did you expect?"

Cheryl was a sophomore in high school when she was raped by a boy on the football team. She went to his house to study with him, and he raped her there. Later, she went to her doctor with a urinary tract infection. He knew what had happened, but he was the football team's doctor and he covered it up. "It was a small-town conspiracy," Cheryl told me matter-of-factly. "I told my mother something happened. My mother at that point could not handle anything. She was dealing with divorce. I didn't want to talk about it at church, where everyone knew me and the jock. I was considered kind of weird anyway, so why would they believe me? I was bipolar and hypoglycaemic, but no one knew what was wrong with me. And on top of it all, we lived in a small Midwestern town."

Years later, their paths crossed again in California.

"I got a file on my desk and it had his name on it. I told my boss what had happened years ago. My boss asked what I wanted to do. I wrestled with it. I had another supportive co-worker and a great boyfriend. I took on an I'll-show-you attitude, went to work dressed up to the nines. In the elevator, there he was. I said, 'Good morning!' He said, 'Are you … ?' I said yes. We made small talk, then I got out on my floor. Then I went to lunch and had a Bloody Mary, or three. It was really empowering!"

Slowly, the rape has become less of a focus. Cheryl credits time, and supportive people around her who don't blame her for what happened. "I think I'm recovering. I still don't like being touched very much. You get to the point where you don't let it affect you. I blamed myself for a while, and then I just said, no. I did not approve this."

I've already mentioned Busisiwe, who was raped at nine. She really wanted to go to church with her friend in southeastern South Africa. Her mother didn't want her to go but finally relented. The church service was over by the time the girls got there, so they went to the friend's house to watch TV for a while. The friend walked Busisiwe most of the way home. While Busisiwe was walking the rest of the way alone, a man came up to her and asked if there were any shops open. She said no. He asked her to help him find one.

"I said, 'No shop is open. I have to go home, my mother will smack me.' He came to my side and he just touched me and closed my mouth. I can't even scream, I can't get his hands off me. We went into an unbuilt shelter house, and he raped me."

Later, after a kindly stranger took her home, "My mother screamed at me and swore at me." It was her father who arranged transport to get her medical help. Her mother never did come around to supporting her, even after tests showed that Busisiwe had contracted HIV from the rape. She had told Busisiwe not to go out that day; what did Busisiwe expect?

When Egypt's legislative branch, the Shura Council, was questioned about the mob sexual assaults on women in Cairo during the Arab Spring, General Adel Afifi of the council said, "Women contribute one hundred percent in their rape because they put themselves in such circumstances."[41]

Here we are in the twenty-first century, surrounded by miracles of our own making. We've figured out how to see each other on tiny little screens we carry around in our pockets. We've figured out how to make a seventeen-year-old heart beat in a sixty-year-old chest. How to track monarch butterflies from Manitoba to Michoacán. How to map galaxies we can't even see. As a species, we can be pretty awesome. So why is it so hard to figure out where you should or shouldn't put your penis? Or understand that nobody asks to be raped?

7

Oh, please

I felt like a bum. I felt like a dirty outcast.

—Dulcie, raped as a child

WHEN I STARTED writing this book, I had no idea of the #MeToo tsunami that was waiting around the corner. I have watched, read, listened, with astonishment and pride, as women all over the world come forward to share their stories and try to find peace and justice.

Larry Nassar treated hundreds of girls and young women for sports-related issues. Many of the American gymnasts we have watched and applauded in the Olympics were under his care, under the auspices of Michigan State University and the US Olympic Committee. Both organizations were informed about multiple instances of sexual abuse, but took no action.[42] The first complaint against Nassar was made more than twenty years ago—in Michigan, in 1997.[43] His career continued to thrive, and presented him with plenty of opportunities to continue committing sexual crimes. He preyed on his clients. He preyed on the six-year-old daughter of a friend. He preyed on whoever he could find. He hurt hundreds of girls and women, as well as at least one young man, and learned again and again that he could get away with it…until one day he couldn't. In 2016, he was indicted on federal pornography charges. Girls and women started to come forward, and in January 2017 Judge Rosemarie Aquilina of the 30th Circuit Court in Ingham County, Michigan sentenced Nassar to between forty and a hundred and seventy-five years in prison.

She also did something else. She encouraged Nassar's victims to speak at his sentencing hearing. A few turned into dozens, which turned into more than a hundred and fifty, and the world watched, riveted, as young women came forward one by one to face their tormentor and detail what had happened to them. It was mesmerizing, horrifying, inspiring, heartbreaking, and deeply moving. Judge Aquilina called the survivors "superheroes."[44]

Lest we think all women are superheroes, let's keep it real by remembering all the drivel that also emerged during this time. Consider the weird little pocket of self-loathing that came out of France, with letters from icons like Catherine Deneuve,[45] and support from scholars like Agnès Poirier, who begs man-hating American feminists to keep their nasty little ideas away from Frenchwomen, who have a "harmony" in their relationships with men that they would like to preserve.[46] Tell that to the fifty-three percent of Frenchwomen who report that they have suffered sexual harassment or assault.[47] Or, for another example, in one *Washington Post* op-ed[48] begging ladies to be reasonable, the writer informs us that men will be men. She assures us that the patriarchy has never done anything to her. Lucky her. She exhorts us to return to business as usual before any more valuable masculine careers are damaged.

As for those valuable masculine careers, and all the wonderful things we lose if we bring great men down, I think our blinkered minds can't even comprehend all we could gain if women were free to reach up and out without fear.

There's a subversive little thread that often weaves itself into any discussion of women actually speaking out and taking space to claim their histories of sexual violence. It's an insidious thread that has choked us for far too long. I call it the Lose-Lose Rape Conundrum. It unwinds like this. If you talk about it, you're a helpless victim angling for sympathy. If you're not a helpless victim, then it wasn't such a big deal, so why are you talking about it? If you're surviving and living your life, why are you ruining some poor man's life? Either it's a big deal, so you're ruined, *or* it's not a big deal and you should be quiet.

Take a look at the videos of Nassar's victims speaking out, and I dare you to call any of them helpless victims. The moment we speak up, the moment we say, "This happened to me. I stand here before you, alive," we stop being victims. So I continue to scratch my head at the women, and men, who insist on abiding by the Lose-Lose Rape Conundrum.

As for the lives of men being ruined by women's openness (and keep in mind, please, that most survivors— male, female, genderqueer, straight, gay, young, old—in the world are still silent, still alone, still keeping their terrible secrets), let's get real. Sexual predators deserve due process, but they don't deserve blanket immunity from accusations any more than any other criminals. *Women's* lives, families, and careers have been damaged for far too long by the silence that has protected sexual violators. And not just women's lives—millions of male rape victims pay an equally high price, and live with their own toxic secrets buried in shame and fear. The ongoing saga of sexually predatory priests in the Catholic Church is just one egregious example.

For anyone whose main concern in all this is the subjugation of men rather than the liberation of women, I have some advice: grow a pair. Of eyes. I don't think we need to worry too much about the imminent avalanche of ruined men falling from on high. Plenty of them get passes. You need look no further than 1600 Pennsylvania Avenue.

8

How to save a life

For a naked man to drag a shrieking, clawing man-eater forth from a window by the tail to save a strange white girl, was indeed the last word in heroism.

—Edgar Rice Burroughs, *Tarzan of the Apes*

WHEN AUDREY phoned from Rome and told her friends what had happened to her, they flew straight to her from different parts of the world without a moment's hesitation.

When an unnamed woman (#LionMama) in South Africa heard that her daughter had been raped, she killed the rapist.[49]

When a High Court judge in Punjab and Haryana read a victim statement about the men who raped her, he decided she was promiscuous and rescinded their sentences.[50]

When a twelve-year-old in Pakistan told her mother she had been raped, her mother went to the village elders, who ordered the rape of one of the rapists' sisters.[51]

When my father found me, he wrapped me in his arms, carried me up four sets of stairs to the roof, and said, "What do you want? We'll do whatever you want."

Four years later, when I was counseling survivors, training professionals, and speaking at schools, I found myself using my father—a middle-aged Muslim man who had never studied psychology, sociology or gender dynamics—as the textbook model for how to behave with a survivor.

It's a simple formula. Give unstinting control, acceptance and support. That's it.

A couple of days after the rape, I got ready to go take a bus to a different part of town. My father came in, saw my bright pink and blue silk shirt, and said, "Don't wear that on the bus!"

"*Arre*, why not?"

"I don't know … people might see you!"

We stared at each other, both horrified at what he had said. I understood that he wasn't ashamed of me. He wanted to protect me, to make me invisible so that nobody could see me, and hurt me.

"Let them see me!" I said.

"Yes, let them."

Then there was the uncle who first didn't want to call the police, then didn't want to tell my mother, then didn't want anyone to talk about it, ever. Once again, my father, usually the decisive one, turned to me for a cue.

"It's not a secret," I fumed. "Why should I hide it, why?"

He took that and ran with it, much to many people's discomfiture. All he wanted was for me to feel better and get whatever I needed. A few days later, we were paying a social call to some people we didn't know very well, who had no idea what had so recently happened. In the middle of tea and biscuits and a totally unrelated conversation, my father suddenly broke in with, "My daughter was raped!" Talk about a conversation-killer … I still laugh when I think about that moment.

Despite the simple formula, it's not always easy to decide what to do. We are always looking for reasons to play down sexual assault. And one of the easiest reasons is plain old discomfort. One woman told me about an uncle groping her, and how she still socialized with him until he died many years later. Shunning him would have meant hurting her aunt, whom she loved. Always making sure there was a table between her uncle and her was easier than creating a huge schism in the family. She and her parents agreed on this. But it's a slippery slope—suppose she had not been able to bear family gatherings? For her, it was not a huge deal to see the creepy old man. For someone else, it might have been.

Mordechai Jungreis, an ultra-Orthodox Jew, belongs—or belonged—to New York's close-knit Orthodox community. The community looks after its own, and lives by strict rules. When he found out that his teenage son who had a learning disability was being molested in a ritual bathhouse, he complained. The alleged molester was arrested. Jungreis was immediately shunned by his community. People stopped speaking to him and his family. He lost his apartment.[52] In Australia, Manny Waks faced similar resistance. Born in Israel, he moved to Australia when he was a small child, and grew up to talk about his own victimization in the context of rampant abuse in the Orthodox Chabad community. He was ostracized, and so traumatized by his community that he left the country. He eventually received a formal apology from his childhood yeshivah, and continues to shine a light on hidden sexual abuse.[53]

In an interview, Jungreis said, "Try living for one day with all the pain I am living with. Did anybody in the Hasidic community in these two years, in Borough Park, in Flatbush, ever come up and look my son in the eye and tell him a good word? Did anybody take the courage to show him mercy in the street?"[54]

But someone did stand up for the boy—his father. Orthodox Jews, religious Muslims, Catholic parishes, software companies, close-knit families—the level of denial of sexual abuse is staggering in so many organized groups. But change can start with one person, one parent.

Manassah Bradley was suicidal in his twenties, years after being raped as a child. Filled with despair and out of hope, he decided to go to a hospital emergency room and tell them he was a rape survivor and needed help. "I said to myself, if they help me, I won't kill myself. If they don't, I will," he told me. "I walked in, in a deep dark place, and told a nurse. She said, 'I believe you.' Those three words kept me from killing myself."

Too many people remain silent about rape and turn their backs. But many don't. Some face the pain, they witness it, they try to change things. These people fascinate me. I've encountered quite a few.

Mitali Ayyangar spent six months in South Sudan with Médecins Sans Frontières (MSF). Sitting with a cup of tea on my flower-filled New York balcony, she conjured up Bentiu Camp, seven thousand miles away. The camp is officially called an UNMISS PoC site (UN Mission in South Sudan: Protection of Civilians). An area of about two-thirds of a square mile is temporary home to what was then about 120,000 people. Mitali managed a team of eighty local community workers, a fourth of whom were women.

Her team's job was to try and keep track of the community's health needs. MSF runs a secondary healthcare hospital and, among various services, they also provide medical help for rape victims; part of Mitali's job was to identify people who needed this help and to raise awareness in the community about rape.

The hospital had a gate called the Yellow Flower Gate, which was exclusively for women. It was a special place for women to come with any issues, not just sexual abuse. "Menses, UTIs, pregnancy-related issues, whatever, no stigma… Most rapes happen to girls and women on their journey to the camp," she explained, "or when they go out to collect firewood."

How to find people who might need help, and offer it to them? Enter the Gate Ladies.

The four Gate Ladies were once traditional birth attendants who came to the camp after fleeing violence in their villages. At the gates of the PoC camp, they take shifts. One of them is always at the camp gates. "They are very much in tune, and intuitive," Mitali said. "They see who goes out in the morning and whether something seems off when they return. A shoe missing, a certain look… they chat with them and try to find out if something happened, taking them a little away from the group so they can talk. They educate about PEP (post-exposure prophylaxis for HIV) and the morning-after pill. If the person agrees to go to the hospital, the Gate Ladies offer to accompany her. At the hospital, staff provide confidential medical care.

"The Gate Ladies are very creative and persistent. They have the right balance between giving space and being there. Women often say, 'They robbed me, but didn't rape me.' Then—maybe they say that they got slapped around.

Then they might say they were raped. It can take a long time."

The Gate Ladies are the core of the program. In general, rape is understood as something that happens at gunpoint. They help spread the message that sexual assault is much more than that—it can happen in families, it doesn't have to involve a penis, etc. They get formal training but there's also a lot of sitting around and talking about MSF's position and how to reconcile it with their beliefs that might be different.

Mitali did her part by learning a song about rape and singing it in Nuer. The song mentions unwanted sexual contact and suggests getting help:

Mi ce tuok wer ke peth, rey nini dok ka em-thep thwok
Rek man in dixk dien min te ke ken mi yian en no
    mo mi thok
Mace din yen e kiim, thile ram bi je mjac.

If this has happened, don't delay! Go quickly, within three days, to MSF (em-thep) at Maternity Gate Three which has a yellow flower. When this happens, you know it—and the doctor or midwife. No one else will know it.

Mitali acknowledged that the camp doesn't provide services to male victims. This is an unfortunate global truth —the lack of sexual assault services for men and boys. No matter how insufficient they are for women everywhere, services are worse for men.

I'm in awe of people who, inspired by others' pain, feel moved to change their lives to help. People like Bhagirath Iyer, a continent and ocean away from South Sudan. A finance professional in India, he was so affected by the December 2012 rape and murder that he and some friends began an organization called Make Love Not Scars, reaching out to help victims of gender violence, particularly acid attacks. He told me that he wants to help women regain their dignity after rape and other forms of assault.

Yet another continent and another ocean away from South Sudan, Sean Grover runs therapy groups in New York City. Inevitably, the subject of rape comes up. Sometimes the group is the first place that someone feels safe acknowledging, even to him or herself, that it has happened.

"You don't want to challenge people's defenses too much," Sean told me. "If you help them to feel safe, they will open up. Defenses are necessary. They keep people intact. They're a scaffolding."

I like that way of looking at it: so much more positive than dumping on denial. What is "denial" anyway? It's a negative word for what is often a coping mechanism that works very well. It can be amazingly effective—as in the case of the teenage rape victim I met who did not think she was pregnant until the baby practically fell out of her. You deal with things when you're ready to deal with them. This is not necessarily bad, unless you're on the tracks and denying that the train really is bearing down on you.

On yet another continent, Laila Atshan, a social worker living in Ramallah, works with rape victims in and near Palestine. She told me about a young Iraqi girl she had just met. "She was kidnapped in Iraq for seven months. She was mistreated in every way you can imagine. Everybody was concerned about whether or not she was a virgin. She was almost dying. She thought she didn't deserve to live." Laila, who is blind, used her own example in talking with the girl.

"I used my blindness as an example to show her that people think I'm of no value. But I have a lot of value, and so, I told her, do you." The girl regained her desire to live. Laila said, "She transformed!"

Laila works closely in the Occupied Palestinian Territory with teachers and parents who feel helpless about their lives and frightened for their children. "We can't control checkpoints," she tells them. "But we can control how we are with our children."

Mitali and Laila are witnesses to pain. We all need witnesses to sit with us and go through the pain. We are all witnesses to rape culture. Some of us have been witnesses to actual rape, and that takes a heavy toll. Rape always cuts a swath through many lives.

What does rape do to men who are witnesses and cannot intervene? I have heard story after story that reminds me of my own: rapists who hurt the woman while the man watches, unable to help. The whole scenario is a toxic blend of machismo and cruelty, a neat way of pressing every button related to what it means to be male and female. In every culture, we cling to prescribed expectations of masculinity and femininity, usually to everyone's detriment. This is why trans people are so threatening, and so necessary.

If you want power and control, and all the research says that is what much of rape is about, then, if you manage to rape a woman and bring a man to his knees at the same time, it must be a double victory. And, if you're the man who has to witness the crime, it must be a double devastation—you see someone, maybe someone whom you love, hurt, and you can't do anything about it. If you're into the whole "honor" paradigm, it's a double dishonor. The man (boy, really)—who witnessed my rape loved me. He fought for me and put his own life on the line, but in the end it was a choice of rape or death. The choice was clear, and neither of us has regretted it for a millisecond. Yes, he felt bad that he couldn't prevent the rapes, but not because he was male. He just felt bad; I would too. We were both wounded and we both got through it. When this happens, two people have been traumatized, the person who is raped and the person who has to stand by.

But not everyone sees it that way.

Assad went into the woods with his fiancée, to steal some time together. They were going to be married in two months, but this was the only way they could be alone. While they were there, three men caught and held him, and took turns raping her.

The couple would have kept it secret, but they were both wounded and so had to tell their parents when they got home. Assad's father's first question wasn't about their injuries. "What did you do?" he demanded of his son. His uncles also wanted to know: How could he have let it happen? Why hadn't he protected her?

This was actually a relatively enlightened response given what could have happened. Another family might have shunned the girl and called off the marriage. But how enlightened was it, really? It's still all about honor, about men's duty to protect women from other men. Women are still there to be taken by the strongest. Assad wasn't the strongest, so he was less of a man. The rapists efficiently dishonored her and emasculated him at the same time.

Most people are neither heroes or rapists. But, sometimes, some people go beyond witnessing. They carry the burden or rush in to intervene. These people are heroes.

Yasmin El-Rifae is one of the founders of OpAntiSH (Operation Anti Sexual Harassment). In 2012, she and other

Egyptian residents were appalled at the mob assaults on women in Tahrir Square, Cairo. During the Arab Spring, groups of men would surround women who were out protesting. After isolating a woman, they would join together to hurt her, anything from grabbing and groping to raping with knives. OpAntiSH mobilized and went out to intervene.

The group conducted outreach on the streets, set up a hotline, and used social media to mobilize teams of men and women equipped with flares, and clothing for victims whose own might have been ripped off. They trained members in non-violent intervention and connecting with victims. More than anything, they trained them to believe that good can short-circuit evil.

I watched an online video of one of the mass sexual assaults. Groups of men screaming, shouting, shoving—a chaotic gathering with a grim purpose. I thought of the emails I got calling me brave for speaking out in an era of silence, and how wrong all those people were. I was frightened just looking at this.

I met Yasmin in Washington Square Park in Manhattan's West Village. We sat on a bench in the summer twilight as she calmly described the strategy and practice of choosing to put herself in danger to save other women. What a hero. Whenever I get overwhelmed by the evil in the world (and I don't use the world lightly, having looked into the face of evil and felt its breath on my face), I remember that its opposite exists too, in people like Yasmin and her group. Imagine going out, putting your life at risk, plunging into a mob, to try and help a total stranger.

Yasmin told me about the group: how they came together, how some of them were raped themselves in the process of intervening, how they trained themselves like warriors to make their way through a snarling chaotic mob and reach a woman in danger.

In one section of Yasmin's manuscript about the feminist resistance to mob sexual assault during the Egyptian revolution, a woman is sitting with another woman, who has just been assaulted:

She knows in her innermost heart-brain that her job will be to never ever leave this woman. They will be skin to skin. She is no longer a person who has come to help Mariam; instead she and Mariam are a unit, and they will make it out together or not at all.

Busisiwe, who was raped as a child, told me how she got home from the building site where she was raped. "Another lady was staying there. She asked the guy, 'What are you doing in the night?' The rapist just told her, 'Just go, just go, do your cooking.' She went. I screamed, and after he finished raping me another grandma was drunk and she called some people. I was all blood and they took me home."

In Sangli, Maharashtra, sex workers are vulnerable to abuse and worse from their customers and neighbors. Three decades ago, a woman named Meena Seshu arrived in their midst. Through SANGRAM (Sampada Gramin Mahila Sanstha), the rural women's rights organization she leads, local sex workers realized that they are each other's best supports. In a culture that refuses to recognize that someone who sells sex for a living can be violated, they are there for each other. One woman demonstrated the way they can bang on the wall and get help if a client gets too rough. Two men told me they would have committed suicide after being assaulted if it weren't for their fellow sex workers and friends. They remind each other that sex work is work, look out for each other's children, and keep each other both safe and sane.

Help comes in all shapes and sizes. Sometimes it's your college professor who sits sympathetically by your side when you have a complete unexplained meltdown in his office. Sometimes it's the people who know what you're talking about because they've also been through it. And sometimes it's a drunk grandma.

9

The Abdulali guidelines
for saving a rape survivor's life

I SAY "she," but the guidelines apply equally to all genders.

- Be horrified, but don't fall off your chair so that she has to take care of you.
- Believe her. No ifs, ands, or buts. Just believe her.
- Let her take the lead. If she wants to talk, okay. If she wants to be quiet, okay. If she wants to cry, okay. If she wants to joke, okay. If she wants to throw things, okay.
- Ask her what she wants. No need to guess.
- Encourage her to get help—medical, legal, physical, mental. But don't force it.
- Don't ask her for details, but let her know you're open to listening if she wants to elaborate.
- Don't question her judgement.
- Let her frame it the way she wants, in the words she chooses.
- Don't try to understand and analyse. Just be there.

- Remember this is the same person you knew before you knew she was raped. Treat her the same. Something terrible has happened to her, but she is the same person. She might also need reminding of this.
- And, last but not least, I could give no advice better than Caitlin Moran's: don't be a dick.

10

The official version

It is absolutely essential to carefully measure the ingredients and follow the recipes faithfully. Without this, perfection is impossible.

—Digvijaya Singh, *Cooking Delights of the Maharajas*

As a man, I apologize for what those evil men did. All of us men are guilty in some way or the other for these atrocities and crimes against our dear women. I hope you have a very happy life and future.

—email, 2013

THE FIRST TIME I got called for jury duty in New York, I was in the pool of potential jurors for a rape trial. About two hundred of us filled the courtroom, and the judge asked anyone who had either been sexually assaulted or known anyone who had been sexually assaulted to raise their hands.

This was in 2009, when rape was much less frequent or open a topic of conversation than it is now. Many hands went up.

We were called into a small room, one by one. I walked in, and found myself at a table with: the judge (a man), the alleged rapist (a man), the defense lawyer (a man), and the prosecuting lawyer (a man). The accused looked dully at me. I avoided his eyes; the room suddenly seemed much smaller.

So, they asked me, tell us about anything in your history that might be relevant to this case. I told them whatever I could remember: I had been assaulted, I had worked at a rape crisis center, I wrote my undergraduate thesis on rape in India, I wrote my graduate thesis on media coverage of rape, I was currently in the midst of helping write a report on election-related rape in Zimbabwe …

The defense lawyer could barely contain himself. I think he was sitting on his hands to keep from pushing me out of the room. The prosecuting attorney smiled at me and asked if I thought I could be objective if I were on the jury.

"Absolutely!" I said. And meant. They didn't ask me to explain, because they didn't have time. The words practically shot out of the defense attorney's mouth—he wanted to use one of his vetoes to kick me off. And that was that. No jury duty for me.

The defense attorney was wrong. I could have been objective. After a lifetime of seeing the terrible damage that lies and assumptions do, I am convinced I would have been fair, and careful not to convict the wrong person. I knew this stuff. I knew all about the justice system and how it is stacked against people of color (the rapist was a man of color). I knew that, in the US, men of color who aren't guilty might plead guilty to reduce their sentences. I knew that, whether you're a victim or a rapist, your caste or class affects every single thing about whether you are believed, and what happens to you. I knew that the second you become part of any institution anywhere in this world, it's no longer about two people. The weight of history, of layers and layers of bigotry and assumptions and rationalizations, all come down on you with irresistible force. To be a black man in America accused of raping a white woman—this is never just about sexual violence. To be a Dalit or a tribal or a Muslim in India and be accused of raping an upper-caste woman—this is never just about sexual violence. I remember, after I was raped, trying to process the knowledge that, if I did decide to press charges, I could go out and point to any poor young man in the local slum, and guarantee him at least a hearty beating at the police station.

But in the US legal system, if you are invested, informed and interested in your subject, you're not fit to judge your peers. If you've been raped, then you can't have an opinion about it because you're too biased, too emotional, too close to it.

Yes, I know. Crazy. But true.

So who gets to judge, what is objectivity, and how do we set our standards? If only people who have had no experience with sexual assault get to sit on juries, it's no wonder the conviction rate in American rape trials is abysmal. Consider this: out of every 1,000 rapes,

- 310 are reported to the police;
- 57 lead to an arrest;
- 11 get referred to the court system;
- 6 rapists go to jail. [55]

The defendant in that 2009 case was, in the words of a man who did serve on the jury and talked to me about it afterwards, "so obviously guilty that on the second day he just gave up and took a plea." But, if he hadn't, would the trial have been fairer with nobody on the jury who had any idea about the nuances of rape? Nobody asked the people on the jury if they had ever *committed* rape. For all I knew, they kicked me off and put on a panel of abusers.

We persist in thinking that, if this has happened to you, you're never quite trustworthy in the same way again. Granted, the same thing happens in other trials—if you've been robbed, you might get disqualified from a robbery case. But the defense attorney probably wouldn't look at you as though you might reach over the table any moment and strangle his client.

I, and many others, have written about the limits of the law to create change. Examples are depressingly ubiquitous. In Somalia, in 2016, the Puntland region passed a comprehensive sexual violence law that was internationally lauded. The existence of such a law is surely a necessary part of the solution. Sadly, however, it is being broken constantly by the very people who are supposed to enforce it. Rapes by the military and police continue unabated.[56]

Change begins at home, in our everyday lives and attitudes. The law, even if a rapist is found guilty, can do only so much to support survivors. The law won't hold your hand when you're scared to go out at night. A change in the law won't necessarily cause a change of heart if you feel passionately about something.

But laws guide our behavior, even if they don't always guide our thoughts. It matters that Sharia law requires the eyewitness evidence of four grown men to prove rape. It matters that statutes of limitations put time limits on reporting sexual abuse. It matters that rape shield laws in the US prevent defense attorneys from talking about victims' previous sexual history in the courtroom. Justice systems are imperfect constructs, but they matter. Laws can and do affect the way we act.

Consider vaccination. Many people think routine inoculations are harmful. In recent years, California experienced several dangerous outbreaks of measles. The state tightened regulations, making it more difficult for parents to exempt their children from being vaccinated. As a result, people simply vaccinated more and the incidence of measles declined significantly. Maybe all these parents still believe that vaccinations are harmful, but the cost of avoiding them went up, and tipped the scales of their decision-making.

Rape is not measles, and there is no vaccination. But rules matter. How do we define rape? What is the burden of proof? How are doctors and police officers trained to handle rape cases? How does sentencing work? How does social media affect due process? Laws won't end rape, but they have deep consequences, and they set a tone.

So does the way we talk about things. Like law, language carries weight. Who came up with, "Sticks and stones may break my bones, but words will never hurt me"? Sticks, stones, words—they can all pierce the skin and the spirit.

The language we use says a lot about our so-called objectivity. Here is an excerpt from the UNDP's guide to HIV-related language.[57] It works for any stigmatized topic:

> *Language and the image it evokes shape and influence behaviour and attitudes. The words used locate the speaker with respect to others, distancing or including them, setting up relations of authority or*

of partnership, and affect the listeners in particular ways, empowering or disempowering, estranging or persuading, and so on.

"The public prosecutor... told me to stop crying and focus," said Audrey. The men who raped her were acquitted, and she still wonders if it was because of the way she gave evidence.

It is amazing that survivors continue to take responsibility for rapists walking free when a) they committed the crime, and b) the system universally sucks. Trials take time. Courtrooms are brutal. Evidence is tricky. Sexual violence isn't a priority. In the US, thousands of rape kits (the packets of forensic evidence containing semen, hairs, fibres, etc. collected from victims) are gathering dust awaiting testing while rapists go free.

The law all too easily distorts and muddles and gets it wrong. The official version is open for interpretation. Look at me: I'm writing this book about rape, but, in the official record, nothing happened to me up on the mountain. It shouldn't matter to me, when I know what happened, but it does. I would give a lot to find that ledger and rewrite the report.

The official version matters. Sticks and stones may break my bones, and words too will always hurt me.

11

Your love is killing me

It's just a hot mess.

> —Gina Scaramella, executive director,
> Boston Area Rape Crisis Center

Sex ed and rape ed—they're one and the same.

> —Jaclyn Friedman

WHEN MY DAUGHTER was in third grade, she didn't like going anywhere with the rest of the class. Walking down the stairs in school on the way to the cafeteria for lunch, trekking up the block and crossing the street to have recess in Tompkins Square Park—she complained about anything that involved getting into her assigned place in the line. What's the big deal? we wanted to know. It turned out that the boy who was always behind her constantly pulled her hair.

"And he blows on me!" she said indignantly.

It seemed fair enough for her to be upset that he didn't stop even when she objected. I mentioned it to her teacher, who laughed and said, "Oh, that's Ted! He has a huge crush on her. That's just his way of showing her he likes her."

Oh, that Ted. He likes her so it's okay.

It's not okay! Someone needs to tell Ted that you don't annoy girls to show them you like them. When Ted goes to college and has an unrequited crush, how's he going to show it? Ask for a movie date? Or break into the woman's room and rape her?

Rape and desire, violence and sex. They're all so mixed up. Maybe they shouldn't be, but they are, and it's a tricky overlap.

What is the connection between rape and desire? Feminist analysis in the West has been so careful about separating the two, about defining rape as an act of violence. Which it is. When I worked at the Boston Area Rape Crisis Center, my friend Irene Metter and I held many workshops for different groups. We had a great time, driving around in her giant blue boat of a car, going to schools, clinics, various offices, talking to groups about different aspects of sexual assault. My favorite sessions were in schools, where we would show up and dive into heated discussions with teenagers. Irene had a line that I loved: "Rape is not sex. If you hit someone on the head with a rolling pin, it's not cooking." It worked really well to illustrate that, while rape might sometimes look like consensual sex, it isn't.

But rape is *sexual* violence.

A sexually frustrated boy taking out his pent-up emotions on a vulnerable girl or a soldier attacking a woman as part of a war: both are rape, both are violent, but do they come from the same place? And does it matter, especially to the victim? How do we parse out the dynamics of date rape and violent stranger rape when we talk to our sons, so that we can admit nuance without diminishing the wrongness of both? While I don't have any answers (again), I do think it's important to keep all these nuances in mind.

Gina Scaramella is executive director of the Boston Area Rape Crisis Center, the same place that hired me in 1984 to be its first full-time staff member. Those were the Wild West days, when they were located in the Cambridge Women's Center, we roared off in the middle of the night to women's homes when they were in danger or frightened, and I once counseled someone on the crisis hotline while dousing the curtains that had caught fire. These days it is a professional organization with forty full-time people and strict rules about showing up at people's homes. But some things haven't changed at all. Rape is still simple (no consent = rape) and still complicated (What is consent? How do you define force? What is power?).

"There are almost no truths," Gina told me. Well, there are some. It's true that if you have sex with someone and he/ she doesn't want it, that's a problem. But it is complicated when you try to assign degrees of blame. "We have to be really clear about that. Everything matters—the age of both victim and perpetrator, their relationship... It all impacts what happens next. Everything falls from there. Everyone wants to simplify, every single time, but we can't. We miss opportunities to intervene when we keep trying to label things," she insisted.

This is so tricky. As counselors and activists, the staff at crisis centers want above all to serve their clients. But they also want to draw clear political lines about what is and isn't acceptable, what is and isn't criminal. That's where the connections between violence, desire and agency are so important.

A young woman in Australia shared a letter she wrote to a man, a friend, after he violated her boundaries. Here are some excerpts:

> *Although I know your intentions were not to harm, it's important for me that you read this letter with care and with empathy…*
>
> *I'm writing to you for two main reasons:*
>
> *1. I want you to realize and truly understand the impact that your actions have had (and are still having) on me.*
>
> *2. I want to do what I can to ensure no other woman has to experience what I did.*
>
> *I felt it was quite clear who was to sleep where: you three boys in the bunk-bed room, and me in the room with the double bed by myself. When you requested and then insisted on sleeping in the double bed too (because you "need to spread out"), a part of me felt awkwardly pushed into a corner; however, another part of me felt trusting so I said yes. I remember my gut feeling a little suspicious and apprehensive at the time, which explains why I set down boundaries and said to you "but no touching," to which you agreed…*
>
> *When you and I got into bed and you got up close to me, I immediately felt disrespected as your host and as your friend. I felt generally uneasy and uncomfortable about the situation.*
>
> *When your hands started freely touching my body, underneath my clothes, I felt disrespected and*

disregarded as a woman and, again, as your friend. I felt grossed-out, uncomfortable and increasingly worried.

When I removed your hands off of my body, and slowly maneuvered away from you along the bed, I felt relieved for a few moments when you did not make a move and I had some space. This only lasted a few moments.

When you came up close to me again, your hands moving quickly all over my body, I felt so unbelievably scared—I remember becoming stiff to the bone. This would explain why I didn't move much. I remember noticing your pants were half down. (Although I was intoxicated, like you, I was very alert and highly aware of what was going on.) You were making moves to get on top of me, while simultaneously attempting to remove my underwear. It all felt so quick to me. My mind and my heart were racing...

Please understand—this was so unbelievably concerning, alarming and fucking terrifying! My "no" was not being heard, and if I'm not being listened to now then how far is this going to go? What else is there for me to do when "no" means nothing? I don't want this... I felt abused...

To me, my body language was a clear sign of disinterest and rejection. I'm communicating that my body is closed to you. You ignored that by trying again and again. That's fucking scary... That made me feel assaulted. These repeated actions by you triggered the scariest thought I've ever had run through my head: "maybe I'll just sleep with him and get it over with and done with"...

After the trip, you had the nerve to personally message me with this: "thanks for having a joke about my drunken actions, it's nice knowing you still had my back though I need to somehow make it up to you" ...

I didn't let your comment slide because "I have your back", I let it slide because I have MY back ... I expect you to take responsibility for your actions. I also want to be reassured, and to be able to trust, that you will not ever hurt anyone else the way you have hurt me ...

I hope you can appreciate how enormously impacting this experience has been for me.

He replied:

This letter made me cry, I'm sorry I made you feel like this. I'm sorry I betrayed your trust and I'm sorry I can't go back in time to protect you from this person. I know I get reckless when I'm drunk but I didn't know I was this reckless. It's truly a stab to my heart that I did that to you, because I really do love you like I love all my friends.

A day late and a dollar short, but he did get the message. It's just unfortunate that the woman here had the double burden of being the victim *and* the educator. And that this story is so common. We've all been there—with the guy who just doesn't get it that We. Are. Not. Interested. Or just doesn't care because he's too drunk or too disrespectful or he's been taught all his life that Dick Conquers All.

One of the many conversations swirling around the #MeToo movement focused on the account of a woman who went public about an uncomfortable sexual encounter with

Aziz Ansari, a well-known comedian.[58] She immediately got slammed for diluting the conversation—why, some people wanted to know, was this celebrity-chasing young woman inserting her story of a drunken escapade into a discussion of *real* harassment and abuse? Were women taking all the mystery and fun out of sex? (I've already expressed my opinion that, when sex has less terror and trauma attached to it, it will be more, not less, alluring.)

How does this all fit together? The Aziz Ansari story illustrates exactly how complicated it can all get, and how quickly. The woman did not call it rape. She did say he penetrated her with his finger, against her wishes. That's legally rape. But is it the same as if he broke into her bedroom, threw her on the bed, and penetrated her with his penis? It's *not* the same. But, to me, the more interesting issue is the way people talked more about her behavior than his. Should she or should she not have spoken out? Should she or should she not have remained anonymous? Should she or should she not have gone home with him?

Arre! Who cares? A man forced himself on a woman and she verbalized her discomfort. Isn't that the point of the story? Are we saying that the victim's behavior somehow lessens the crime? That goes against every notion of putting responsibility where it belongs.

Maybe the most significant part of the story is that it *is* a story. I have no idea if the #MeToo movement will prevent a single instance of stranger rape or rape in war. I am sure, however, that these difficult conversations are important among people who have to live with each other every day. One male friend said to me that he is re-examining his life and relationships, and feels uncomfortable about some of the assumptions he has made about women. This man is not a rapist. But he had never thought about what it means to simply assume that, unless a woman explicitly says no, it's okay to unzip and go for it. Another told me he feels lucky—not virtuous, but simply lucky that, despite not having these nuances articulated for him a generation ago, he was never in a situation at which he now looks back with shame at his own behavior.

Bad sex is awful. Bad sex is not rape, but sometimes it ends that way. But are they related? Yes! No! Sometimes! And there is much in between: after reading the Aziz Ansari letter, I hesitate to call it simply "bad sex." The story sounds dehumanizing and denigrating—an entitled man with absolutely no concern for his companion's wishes—and depressingly, demoralizingly familiar. It absolutely belongs in the conversation. The conversation is complicated.

A bad sexual experience for a man is more likely to be a missed communication, some sexual frustration and a sour aftertaste, whereas for a woman the menu is statistically more likely to include humiliation, pregnancy, rape and death. I'm not sure why someone should be shamed for talking about bad sex. We have the internet now, with unlimited space for unlimited rantings and ravings. Talking about one thing doesn't have to take space from the other. Instead, it might help make sense of the "hot mess."

Jaclyn Friedman has a podcast called *Unscrewed*.[59] I spoke with her about sex education in the US. She was scathing. "Either we preach abstinence-only, or we do what I call disaster-prevention sex ed." Disaster-prevention sex education tells young people that you really shouldn't have sex, but, if you insist, then do x, y, and z to protect yourself. "It leaves out the idea that sex should feel good for women. That should be taught to girls *and* boys."

She remembers that, when she was in school, the anatomy diagrams in her sex ed. class didn't include the clitoris. "They left it out because sex was not supposed to be about pleasure." These days the clitoris has fans in all sorts of places. In Sangli, India, adolescents in sexuality workshops learn to call it the "Kama Sutra Kendra (room)."

"If we leave pleasure out of sex ed., we normalize sexual assault," Jaclyn insists.

She has a very good point. Girls and boys get completely different messages about sex. We assume that sex feels good for boys, but girls learn early that losing their virginity is supposed to hurt. We create the idea that sex is uncomfortable for girls, and we raise girls who don't think they deserve pleasure, and boys who at best don't care about their partners' pleasure, and at worst are actively abusive.

In this day and age of gender fluidity, increased acceptance of alternate sexualities, and LGBTQ+ liberation, these parameters should seem increasingly stifling and damagingly heteronormative, but they flourish. And so does rape. We raise our children with such unclear standards that they don't even have the tools to recognize rape when they see it. We really have a problem if we think it's easy to confuse sex with rape.

Jaclyn has a stark example of this:[60]

I think often of the two men who intervened when they came upon Brock Turner assaulting an unconscious woman at Stanford—they knew instantly that something was wrong, because she was clearly not participating. Contrast that with Evan Westlake, who in high school witnessed his two friends raping a semi-conscious girl at a party in Steubenville, Ohio. When asked why he didn't intervene, he told the court, "Well, it wasn't violent. I didn't know exactly what rape was. I always pictured it as forcing yourself on someone."

I'm sure there are many differences between Westlake and the two men in the Turner case—and these cases are different from the Ansari situation—but the one that stands out to me is that Westlake was raised here in the US. The two men on bicycles in Palo Alto were Swedes, raised in a country that teaches healthy attitudes toward sexuality and gender in school, starting in kindergarten, including lessons on not just biology but healthy relationships, destigmatizing taboos around sex, and, yes, affirmative consent. They knew that a woman who is lying still and not participating in sex is a woman who isn't consenting. And it prompted them to take action.

"Imagine how different the world could be if girls and women could be the subjects and not the objects of sex!" Jaclyn said.

This was a lightbulb moment for me—after struggling with how to make these connections between rape and sex without betraying a lifetime of separating them in my mind, I finally understand: you can only separate them when you view them together. I understand exactly what Jaclyn meant when she said, "The idea that you can talk about sexual liberation without talking about sexual violence is bankrupt."

Talking about both also does a huge service to rape survivors who too often feel that sexual pleasure is off limits for them after their traumas. As if flashbacks and shame aren't enough, there's the crippling guilt that survivors experience if they are among the minority of victims who have had orgasms during rape. When someone violates your body, and your body betrays you with its own physical response, it's all too easy to cope by simply shutting it off. If survivors feel safe to work through their own particular horror shows while believing they *deserve* to enjoy sex, they will no longer be left out of the conversation and the possibility of healthy sexual lives.

Much of this is relevant to male-on-male rape as well. I remember talking to male survivors on the rape crisis hotline. The shame, the blame, the feeling of being overpowered are exactly the same. Rape in any context is sex that you grab, not sex that you negotiate and mutually enjoy.

At the other end of the world from schoolkids in Boston, grassroots women's organization SANGRAM runs sexuality workshops which are so popular that one year, when they had no funding to pay participants' transport costs, more than a thousand showed up anyway, bicycling long distances from their villages.

Like Jaclyn, Meena Seshu of SANGRAM promotes the radical notion that, if sex isn't good for women, it isn't good. "We teach them about pleasure," she said. "We tell the boys: once you satisfy the women, you don't have to rape them."

I'd be a total fool if I posited that rape would end if all men were to recognize the importance of consensual sexual pleasure. I'm not saying that at all. But I am saying that violence and desire are often uncomfortably intimate with each other.

12

A brief pause for horror

TIME OUT, TIME out. Let's take just a moment to get down and dirty.

I feel the need to remind you that, while this is a book about talking about rape, it's important not to get so comfortable and conversational that we forget something: rape is staggeringly horrible. Most of us survive, and, if we're lucky, get to appreciate the sounds of birds hurling crockery at each other in the trees of a summer morning. But, no matter how much we talk about it, it is in fact staggeringly, almost incomprehensibly awful. Like war, childbirth and other traumas, it's almost impossible to explain if you haven't been through it.

So please, take a moment. Take a moment to try and understand the awfulness of it all before we get back to talking objectively about it. It's important.

I have one terrible fear about this book. It's worse than the fear of ridicule and negative reviews, or the fear of someone saying to me, "You're *still* talking about this?" It's the fear that, in my hopes of contributing to the conversation in a level-headed manner, I will appear to be saying that rape is no big deal. It's the fear that, in saying it does not have to be the end of hope and light, I will appear flippant and not honor rape victims' terrible suffering and trauma. Hence this chapter.

Sometimes people intellectually understand that men can sexually force women, but have trouble comprehending the pain and indignity involved. Perhaps that's because, no matter how hard we scream and yell at Take Back the Night marches, rape does indeed have a lot to do with sex.

It's like sex's evil twin. All the things that make sex wonderful—intimacy, connection, sensation, choice—make rape so horrible and hard to bear. And confusing. What *should* be transcendent isn't. What *should* be a sacred human connection, or even just a fun interaction, isn't. Rape is not a harmless fantasy of violation and domination. It is not a role-play with rules and limits or a titillating fetish. It is real, and it doesn't come with a safe word.

Are you a person who has never had his or her body violated? I hope you never do. But, just for a moment, imagine this. Imagine someone, maybe someone you like, maybe someone you've never met, but someone who has momentary control of you, forces your legs apart, your mouth open, and rams a piece of himself inside the most intimate parts of you, the soft parts, the vulnerable parts, the trusting parts. There you are. You can't move. You can't breathe. You no longer belong to yourself. Maybe you're afraid you'll die. Maybe you're afraid you'll never ever feel good again. Maybe you're right. When you're down there, spread apart, with someone inside you, rape is not a metaphor. It is most definitely physical. It's blood and gore and tipped with poison, and it hurts.

I read an article in the *New York Times*[61] about a girl who shares my name. Souhayla is sixteen years old, and escaped after three years in Mosul when her Islamic State captor was killed. She is Yazidi. She was thirteen when she was taken into captivity, and has spent the last three years being raped constantly and afraid for her life. When she first reunited with her family, she ran to them and hugged them. But soon she stopped speaking. Now she sleeps most of the time, and does not even have the strength to sit up. Doctors who have examined escapees like her have reported "extraordinary signs of psychological injury." She and other escapees lie all day on mattresses, unable to move.

During the first two years of her captivity, Souhayla was raped by seven men. At the beginning of the push for Mosul, she was moved progressively deeper into the conflict area, near the Tigris River. The small patch of land was under fire every day. As the Islamic State began to lose the fight, the man holding Souhayla at the time cut her hair short, like a boy's. He planned to try to slip the two of them, disguised as refugees, past Iraqi security forces.

Souhayla now lives with her uncle, who spends his days nursing her back to health. The *Times* story reports that she could not even sit up unaided. After her escape, "almost two weeks passed before she was able to stand for more than a few minutes, her legs unsteady."

There is a photo of Souhayla accompanying the story. She is sitting in a chair with her head tilted to one side, holding up the polka-dotted cloth that covers her face and head. You can see only her eyes looking off to the left. She is thin but she manages to dominate the photograph. She could be my daughter, who is also sixteen. A fragile seed, with secret powers.

I have read thousands of rape stories, spoken with hundreds of victims, but this photograph of Souhayla instantly flew past all my defenses. It is like a punch in the gut every time I look at it.

That is what you must feel, and remember, while we continue our conversation about rape: that punch in the gut. The blood and gore, the horror, the horror.

13

A bagful of dentures

She reached into her pants and took out a doll.

—Sharonne Zaks, dentist, Melbourne, Australia

THE US National Institute of Mental Health defines post-traumatic stress disorder (PTSD) as "a disorder that develops in some people who have experienced a shocking, scary, or dangerous event."[62] Symptoms include flashbacks and everything else from specific fears to a complete inability to function. Given the level of trauma in the world—war, torture, illness, loss, planetary malaise—I think it's safe to assume that plenty of people are walking around (or staying home with the covers over their heads) with PTSD.

Rape survivors know it well.

If you've been raped in the context of a conflict, either geo-political or in your own bedroom, rape adds insult to the other injuries you suffer. If you've "only" been raped, PTSD can still bring you to your knees.

In my first job, I counseled hundreds of women who were in crisis after rape. Some spoke to me minutes or hours after it happened; some called years, or even decades, later. But they were all in crisis, and, although we were not diagnosticians at the rape crisis center, we could tell that many had symptoms of PTSD. I never did tease out any kind of consistent connection between the particular trauma and the level of PTSD, or how it manifested itself. Human beings are complex, and one person may bounce back quickly from a crime that breaks another's spirit.

Sean Grover counsels soldiers and is always interested in how someone who has seen or experienced relatively little active warfare can be rendered dysfunctional, while someone else might have had a bomb blow up in his face, seen all his colleagues killed, and be fine.

The US Department of Veterans Affairs lists the following reactions to sexual assault:[63]

- Major depressive disorder.
- Anger.
- Shame and guilt.
- Social problems.
- Sexual problems.
- Alcohol or drug abuse.

That's all very well, and I suppose "social problems" can include just about anything, but, as anyone who's been raped—or tortured, or been in a war, or so many other things nobody should experience—knows, it's the weirdest things that can get you. Like dentophobia.

While few people love going to the dentist, a tooth-cleaning visit can hold particular horrors for a rape survivor. The first time after the rape that a man with a mask came at me with sharp instruments while I was lying helplessly in his chair, I almost fled the room. They don't tell you about that in the pamphlets. They don't tell you that you might freeze in a job interview because the man asking you questions is wearing a tie just like the one your rapist wore. They don't tell you that you may dread becoming pregnant because having a child is going to mean you have to pay some serious attention to your vagina, which is historically not a peaceful place ...

So survivors suffer a double whammy. They endure unpredictable phobias, fears and reactions, *and* they think they're crazy because nobody else could possibly feel this way.

When we talk about trauma and recovery, too often we think along set patterns: if someone is raped, sex is complicated, and we might be sympathetic. But rape trauma, like grief, can manifest in so many ways, and make you feel crazy. None of the manifestations is crazy.

I didn't cry much at my father's funeral gathering, but weeks later, when I saw a packet of Oreos in a store, I broke down. That's how it goes. My father loved Oreos. I can read about rape, write about rape, talk about rape, no problem, but for many years the sight of striped pyjamas nauseated me, and the dentist's chair was something I had to psych myself up for every time.

None of it makes sense, but when we talk about rape we have to leave room for that. It doesn't make sense. And that's just how it is.

Sharonne Zaks is a dentist in Melbourne, Australia. It runs in the family: her father and her uncle are both dentists, and she still practises with her uncle, as well as running her own clinic. She has developed a program on trauma-informed care, which she implements in her own work. Helping survivors of all kinds of trauma—war, torture, sexual abuse—get dental care is a "huge passionate mission" for her, she told me. I'm a fan of anyone with the goal of helping survivors.

Thinking about trauma-informed care came naturally to Sharonne. Her childhood was very focused on trauma. All four of her grandparents survived the Holocaust. She grew up watching "stressful" documentaries. When she was six, she had a traumatic experience in a hospital. She was held down, subjected to needles, "and it was all awful." She quickly developed a phobia of doctors, despite having doctors in the family.

"In my practice, the most rewarding relationship is the journey with patients to move through their phobia of dentistry. People's lives can really get turned around," she told me. "Many of my patients in twenty years of practice have been trauma survivors." People come to her through word of mouth and her regular clients travel long distances to see her.

Sharonne sees a massive gap in dentistry, as well as a reluctance among trauma survivors to seek dental care. "As dentists we are not educated about this. And patients tend not to relate the phobia to sexual abuse."[64] In response, she has created videos for both dentists and potential patients. They include practical tips on how to make dental care bearable and positive.

For patients, she also talks about why oral health is important. Often, they haven't been to the dentist for far too long. In addition, many coping or self-medicating behaviors among trauma survivors are centered on the mouth. Too much drinking, too much smoking, too much sugar, too much eating, grinding teeth—all these directly affect your teeth and gums. So trauma and dental hygiene are bound together in dangerous ways. As a trauma survivor, you might be prone to do things that directly hurt your mouth, but, as a trauma survivor, you might be a lot less likely to get help for your mouth *because* you're a trauma survivor. Another insidious side effect.

"We treat anxious patients all the time anyway, but how do we recognize signs of sexual abuse? A lot of anxiety resides in the dentist-patient relationship, *not* the patient," Sharonne explained.

This makes perfect sense to me. Rape survivors crave control. For me, part of that control is language. I use words to adjust my environment. I used words to persuade my rapists not to kill me. One of the worst things you could do to me is immobilize me on a chair and put things in my mouth so that I can't talk.

Sometimes just knowing that someone knows can help. In a photo essay about a visit to Jamaica by Tufts University dentistry students,[65] I saw a still of a young girl with tears streaming down her face before getting her tooth extracted. The dentistry student, Michael Golub, asked her if she had been abused, and she said yes, the scars on her arms were from burning cigarettes. After she had told him, the extraction was quick and there were no more tears.

"The biggest thing that helps people to open up is that, when I first meet them, I just sit and listen," Sharonne told me. "I don't rush them in any way. They set the agenda at the first meeting. I encourage them to say whatever they like, and I believe them. I try to find out what they want and what they know. I encourage them to bring a trusted person or distracting or comfort objects. Or to plan a treat for afterwards. I try not to keep them waiting. I ask them if they want the door open or closed; if they want to bring music. The environment of the surgery is important. Many dental procedures are triggers. Even brushing or flossing are problems. People don't like to put things in their mouths. It's a slow process getting them to start. You have to be patient. It's all about giving control back, with most empathy and least judgement.

"It's just basic compassion, really. You have a huge impact on people's lives as a dentist. You give them skills they can use."

She works the way everyone should. Be open. Listen. Don't assume. Don't take away control.

Anna has been Sharonne's patient for seven years. She is a single mother. She was abused as a child. Recently she told Sharonne, "Don't ever underestimate your impact, Sharonne Zaks. Coming to you has helped me feel that I'm worthy."

It renewed Sharonne's faith that her attention to detail is worthwhile. "You just don't know what impact you have. We think it's all aesthetics and health—you help someone chew again, etc. We forget about the psycho-social elements."

Of course, as with any painful human drama, her work has its funny side. One patient who acts out to feel comfortable walks into the surgery yelling, "Shut the fuck up and treat me!" One patient sings to remain calm. She sings non-stop, even with water and instruments in her mouth. She is trained in opera, and has such a great voice that people gather outside the door to listen. Another patient also illustrates the power of music, which really deserves its own chapter. She refused to open her mouth for the dentist until

Sharonne discovered (from her accompanying carer) that she loves Madonna. Now Sharonne is the proud owner of every Madonna CD ever made. She sings at the top of her voice and dances as she treats her patient. Now that's dedication.

Another patient with a history of severe sexual trauma had avoided going to a dentist for thirty-five years. She came in wearing a huge bright yellow garment with lots of pockets.

"We were all focused on our work," Sharonne told me. "I was giving her a big filling. All of a sudden, I heard a loud noise coming from under her clothing. The nurse and I didn't know what to do, so we kept going. Then I heard it again: 'I'm your guardian angel!' The patient reached into her pants and took out her talking doll. That was her comfort object."

Dentistry is just one example. Studies have shown that in any circumstances, patients feel less anxious, heal faster, leave hospital settings sooner and generally do better when their health care providers talk with them, answer questions, and are clear about what they can expect from a visit or a procedure.[66]

In a 2017 article, "When Cancer Treatment Re-traumatizes Survivors of Sexual Trauma,"[67] an oncologist and a psychologist wrote about a breast cancer patient, Mary, who was shocked and traumatized by her treatment, starting with the biopsy, which replicated her experience of being helpless as a sexually abused child. The authors write:

> *As we listened to Mary, we were both chilled and heartbroken. And as psychologists, we were chastened. We consider ourselves empathetic, we have worked clinically with many sexual abuse survivors, and as a*

standard part of initial psychotherapeutic evaluations we always ask about a history of abuse. But, in a cancer setting, we were so focused on the diagnosis, the treatment, and the adverse effects of the cancer and its therapy…

Never again. We have had our eyes opened, and we now recognize how many aspects of medically necessary, well-intended, and seemingly sterile clinical procedures could potentially serve as emotional triggers that remind abuse survivors of the original trauma. For example, many oncology procedures involve darkness (e.g. radiology, radiotherapy); exposure of sexual organs (e.g. in breast, gynecological, anal, and prostate treatment); being silenced, immobilized, or powerless (patients often are told not to speak or move during procedures); feeling that you are under someone else's control, someone who can do anything to you that they want (e.g. through anesthesia, through restraints, and through telling you to remain still); penetration (by instruments, needles, hands, fingers); and infliction of pain. All of these are also common features of sexual abuse.

They go on to detail the ways in which medical professionals can be helpful, ask the right questions, and make survivors more comfortable.

There's a pattern here. Doctors come into direct contact with people's bodies, but they are not the only ones who could support sexual violence survivors. Whether you're a teacher, a plumber, a manicurist, a taxi driver, an accountant or a family friend, there's huge value in remembering that everyone you meet has a story, everyone you meet has been hurt in some way. There's huge value in finding out what might or might not aggravate the pain.

There's value in being open to signs that someone is vulnerable, asking when we're in doubt, and remembering that they've had a whole life before they met us, for better or worse. Sometimes worse—like the man with no trousers on the subway the other night who yelled, "Mmmmmotherfucker!" as soon as I got on the train. Sometimes the best way to proceed is to back right out the way you came before the door shuts behind you.

Part of providing comfort and support is recognizing the limits of what you can do. Sharonne treated many Holocaust survivors in her family practice. "They come in with a bag full of dentures, like, fifteen pairs, made by various dentists, and say, 'I've been to all the dentists here and nobody is any good but I have heard that *you* are amazing and wonderful and you are going to solve all my problems. All of these dentures are rubbish!' It isn't about the dentist, it's about a particular kind of attention. What they really want is something—love—and dentistry is just an excuse. They want to be understood."

Don't we all?

14

Teflon Man

To cut a long story short, I was misbehaved with and after I raised the grievance I get victimized and continue to work despite sweet managerial talks that they are looking for a respectful alternative with nothing done. Whereas the villain of the incident goes ahead, denies all charges, buys himself a new car and dressing up in new coats and suits moves around like he is the biggest thing to happen ever.

—email, 2013

HILLARY GOODRIDGE was a freshman at an Ivy League college that had just begun to accept women. During her freshman year, she was happy. She had a sweet boyfriend, she enjoyed her classes, and generally felt good about her life.

She took a large human relations class with a teacher she really liked, one of the few women professors. The class had six or seven women. One of her classmates, a man, was a Native American ex-Marine. He asked Hillary out on a date, and she politely declined, saying she had a boyfriend.

He was disappointed. "He said, 'Just a drink,'" she told me, "and I said, really, no thank you, again."

Hillary is a friend of mine, and a kind person. She hates saying no, but she didn't want to go out with this man.

He said, "Please, just one drink. I don't know how to talk to girls. You're so nice to me. Can't you help me to be better at it? Just one drink in a public place." He had just returned to campus after being in Vietnam. There had been no women at the college when he left.

As I said, she's a kind person. She said okay, and they went out for the drink. He didn't have any money, so she paid. He said he had to pay her back, and she said, no, forget it, it's all right. He insisted that she come to his room, and she said no again.

He said, "Why—don't you trust me?"

So she went.

The minute they got into the room, he switched on some really loud music (she still can't stand to hear that song), slammed her against the wall, and raped her. She screamed but nobody heard, and he put his hands around her throat and strangled her to stop her.

"I had bad bruises from the choking," she told me. "I barely remember the rape, because my biggest fear was that I would be choked to death."

The next day, he sent her a rose.

Hillary told a friend the same day, and went to the dean and a doctor the next day. The dean said there was nothing he could do, but she was welcome to go to the police if she wanted. He said, "But he's an ex-Marine and a Native American. Good luck with that!"

Frustrated and traumatized, Hillary went to her professor, who invited all the girls in the class to her own home. Hillary told them what had happened to her. She couldn't bear the thought of someone else going through the same thing.

One of her classmates went to the rapist and told him that Hillary had spoken out about the attack. He promptly threatened to sue both Hillary and the professor for defamation. So now she was dealing with rape trauma, the anguish of living on the same campus as her rapist, and a possible lawsuit.

She found out much later that the dean had talked to her father, who hired a bodyguard to follow her around. The dean also asked one of her male friends to report back about how she was doing. She didn't find out until later that she had a stalker and a spy. Well-intentioned though it might have been, here were a couple of men deciding what was good for her without checking with her. Did she really need more male power over her life?

It has been decades since the rape, but I know, sitting in a café with Hillary and calmly discussing it, how it never leaves her. Neither of us could imagine whether or not the rapist ever thinks about it, but it never goes away for her, even if she doesn't think about it specifically. I know how tedious it is to decide whom to tell, how to tell, when to tell.

Her rapist was protected by his minority status and military service. He wasn't her boss, but he still had power he could use to intimidate and silence her. Power plays into rape in ways that transcend opportunity and motive.

Power further corrupts everything that is already corrupt about rape:[68] who is believed, who is accountable, who is punished, and why.

In 1997, Jennifer Freyd[69] wrote about betrayal trauma theory, which addresses the dynamics of suppressing memories of childhood abuse. She held that betrayal trauma applies to other situations, such as marital rape.

> *...when a woman feels dependent upon her male partner, some degree of unawareness of the abuse may be adaptive in maintaining an apparently, or actually, necessary system of dependence and attachment.*

Freyd went on to try to understand what happens when a victim or third party openly confronts an observer. She proposed that abusers frequently respond to accusations with "DARVO"—Deny, Attack, and Reverse Victim and Offender:

> *I hypothesize that if an accusation is true, and the accused person is abusive, the denial is more indignant, self-righteous and manipulative, as compared with denial in other cases. Similarly, I have observed that actual abusers threaten, bully and make a nightmare for anyone who holds them accountable or asks them to change their abusive behavior. This attack, intended to chill and terrify, typically includes threats of lawsuits, overt and covert attacks on the whistle-blower's credibility, and so on...the offender rapidly creates the impression that the abuser is the wronged one, while the victim or concerned observer is the offender.*

Two decades later, her words are as timely as ever. DARVO works too well, too often, which is why it is just so satisfying when it doesn't. Now that we're talking of powerful people, consider the story of singer Taylor Swift's brush with sexual harassment.

Swift is idolized by millions of young women. People pay attention to her. Which makes the story of her assault and battery court case that much more pleasing.

Swift accused David Mueller, a radio show host, of lifting her skirt and grabbing her buttock during a 2013 photo shoot. There's even a photograph commemorating the moment. The radio station fired Mueller. Mueller sued Swift (and her mother!) for three million dollars for causing him to lose his job. Swift countersued him for assault and battery, for one dollar.[70] He wanted money; she wanted to make a point.

The transcript of her court testimony is excellent. Mueller's attorney, Gabriel McFarland, deployed DARVO, trying to pin the blame everywhere but on his client, and Swift was having none of it. Her testimony[71] in Colorado district court deserves its rightful place among treatises on gender empowerment.

McFarland: *You contend that Mr Mueller put his hand underneath your skirt and grabbed your bare bottom.*

Swift: *Yes. He stayed latched on to my bare ass cheek as I lurched away from him, visibly uncomfortably.*

McFarland: *Can you describe how you moved away from Mr Mueller?*

Swift: *The three of us were standing in a row, like you would pose for a photo. I felt him grab*

> *onto my ass cheek underneath my skirt. The first couple of milliseconds, I thought it must be a mistake, and so I moved to the side very quickly so that his hand would be removed from my ass cheek, and it didn't let go.*

McFarland: *And you were trying to get as far away from Mr Mueller as you could?*

Swift: *I got as far away from him as I possibly could, being that I was intertwined with two people with my hands on their upper backs.*

McFarland: *Mr Mueller never grabbed your butt outside of your clothing?*

Swift: *He grabbed my ass underneath my skirt.*

McFarland: *So you acknowledge that Mr Mueller never grabbed your butt outside of your clothing.*

Swift: *Rather than grabbing my ass outside of my clothing, he grabbed my ass underneath my clothing.*

McFarland: *And Mr Mueller never otherwise touched your rear outside of your clothing.*

Swift: *He was busy grabbing my ass underneath my skirt, so he didn't grab it outside of my skirt.*

McFarland: *And other than the incident underneath the skirt, Mr Mueller didn't otherwise touch you inappropriately?*

Swift: *Other than grabbing my ass underneath my skirt against my will and refusing to let go, he did not otherwise touch me inappropriately.*

McFarland: *After Mr Mueller exited the photo booth with Ms Melcher, you continued on with the meet-and-greet.*

Swift: *Yes.*

McFarland: *You continued on as if nothing had happened?*

Swift: *As soon as Mr Mueller and Ms Melcher exited the meet-and-greet area, there was another group of fans in the photo booth, and I would have had to say to them, "Excuse me, can you please leave while I talk to my team."*

McFarland: *You think the fans would not have understood that you needed just a couple seconds, so they step out and then they step back in? You think that would have ruined their experience?*

Swift: *I think that when people are excited and they've been waiting in line for hours and they've shown up early for the concert, I don't want to make anything awkward or uncomfortable or make them feel insecure. I want people to have a good time at my meet-and-greets and my concerts. I do not want people to stick their hands up my skirt and grab my ass.*

McFarland: *You could have looked at the next guests and said, "I'm really excited to meet you guys, I just need two seconds."*

Swift: *Yes, and your client could have taken a normal photo with me.*

McFarland: *Do you think it's odd that your personal, professionally trained bodyguard let this big guy get close to you, put his hand under your skirt, grab your butt, stay latched on as you tried to get away, and not do anything?*

Swift: *What Mr Mueller did was very intentional, and the location was very intentional, and it happened very quickly. I wasn't going to blame Greg Dent for something that Mr Mueller did. None of us could have expected this to happen.*

McFarland: *But if Mr Dent was watching and paying attention, do you agree that he had to see you try to get away from him?*

Swift: *I feel like these are questions for him.*

McFarland: *So you're not critical of your bodyguard for allowing Mr Mueller to grope you and then waltz out of the photo booth?*

Swift: *No, I'm critical of your client for sticking his hand under my skirt and grabbing my ass.*

McFarland: *What was your reaction when you learned that Mr Mueller had been fired?*

Swift: *I did not have a reaction.*

McFarland: *You weren't surprised that Mr Mueller was fired.*

Swift: *I just wanted to never have to see him again, and yet here we are, years later, and he and you are suing me, and I'm being blamed for the unfortunate events of his life that are a product of his decisions, not mine.*

McFarland: Do you think Mr Mueller got what he deserved?

Swift: I don't feel anything about Mr Mueller.

McFarland: You don't care about Mr Mueller?

Swift: I don't have any feelings about a person that I don't know.

McFarland: Let's talk about the photo for a minute. You contend that this photograph shows Mr Mueller's hand under your skirt grabbing your bare butt as you're trying to get away.

Swift: Yes.

McFarland: Yesterday we heard from your mom that this dress is stiff like a lampshade, or something like that.

Swift: Yes.

McFarland: Can you explain to me how, given the stiffness of this skirt—if Mr Mueller's hand is actually grabbing your bare cheek in this photograph, why isn't the front of your skirt someplace else?

Swift: Because my ass is located in the back of my body.

McFarland: But the skirt is stiff, so we just talked about when you lift up one side, the whole skirt comes up like a lampshade.

Swift: He didn't lift up the front. He put his hand underneath the back of my skirt, latched on to my ass cheek, and wouldn't let go.

McFarland: In this picture, you're obviously closer to Ms Melcher than you are to Mr Mueller.

Swift: *Yes. She did not have her hand on my ass.*

McFarland: *Ms Swift, have you ever watched police shows?*

Swift: *Yes. I named my cat after detective Olivia Benson from* Law and Order: SVU.

McFarland: *Have you ever wondered why, in the police shows, when they show a lineup, they include five or six guys, they don't put just one in the lineup?*

Swift: *In order to create an accurate lineup for this, we would have had to have other men in the meet-and-greet who had stuck their hand up my skirt and grabbed onto my ass cheek, but there was no one else like this. That was the only person who did that, in my whole career, in my whole life.*

She won the case. And showed us all that you don't have to take the blame. Holding men accountable doesn't mean you're weak; in fact, the opposite is true. Yes, she's rich and famous, but she wasn't immune to being groped by a non-celebrity who was fully confident that he would get away with it.

It's easy and satisfying to denigrate celebrity culture, and to lament the fact that film stars and fashion models steer public opinion through Instagram more than, say, a random academic with deep knowledge. But so what? Who says film stars and fashion models are any more shallow and silly than the rest of us or any of our political leaders? There are some pretty low-wattage "experts" out there, and some highly intelligent celebrities. And, for better or worse, the celebrities have the power to grab headlines. They are definitely part of the conversation. They help set its tone. So I say, *both* Taylor Swift and Mary Beard have earned seats at the table.

Even when there's no overt sexual attack, it's very disconcerting when someone in power steps out of their prescribed role. One of my editors at one of my first journalism jobs had a habit of hugging a little too hard and lingering over the hugs. After a while, I avoided being alone with him. I wasn't traumatized by the minor groping, but it had another insidious effect—it undermined my confidence. This was the man who had given me the job, a prestigious one, and suddenly I found myself wondering whether I was really good enough. Was I qualified for the job, or did he just want me around for a little touchy-feely on the side? Had he used his power to give me a deserved break, or just for fun? Do powerful men have any idea of all the ways they can mess with your mind?

15

Keys to the kingdom

...and so he walked on from day to day, studiously striving to look a man, but knowing within his breast that he was a god.

—Anthony Trollope, *The Warden*

In November 2016, just after the US presidential election, one of therapist Sean Grover's clients, a woman with a family history of sexual abuse, came into his office, crying so intensely that she could barely speak. Many of his clients were similarly affected. "Many women in my groups who fell into depression after the election grew up with an out-of-control or abusive parent. Having a president who made them feel unsafe reawakened their early trauma. Once again they find themselves with a leader who doesn't protect them."

The phenomenon of women reacting so viscerally to the prospect of the man who said "Grab 'em by the pussy"[72] becoming president was reported by the media as well. Politics aside, why did so many people take it so personally and what does this mean about the importance of leadership?

Leaders lead. Presidents, prime ministers, kings and queens, heads of Hollywood studios, CEOs, village patriarchs, school principals, courtroom judges...we look to them to set the standards for the rest of us. We have some awe-inspiring role models, of course (come back, Michelle Obama!) but they are much harder to find.

Silvio Berlusconi, who boasted that he was so busy having sex with underage women that he was only prime minister of Italy in his spare time.[73] The King of Swaziland, who recently married his fifteenth virgin, picked from a line-up of topless young girls.[74] Tycoons who treat women as commodities. Hollywood moguls, who have shown us that all those casting-couch myths weren't myths after all. All over the world, we tend to give powerful men, from national leaders to village elders, a free pass when it comes to their treatment of women.

Rape, of men as well as women, has historically been a handy tool for leaders. Zimbabwe, Bangladesh, Uganda, Cambodia, Bosnia...there's a long list of places where campaigns of sexual violence meant to create terror and abet ethnic cleansing have been explicitly or implicitly encouraged.

Rape as a political tool is one of the many baffling aspects of rape. Consider this oddity, for instance: many cultures tend to value boys more than girls. Yet, if you want to humiliate the men of a culture, your best bet is to rape the women. Boys are worth more, but girls are more worthy of rape. This gets to the core irony of being raped: you're simultaneously not good enough, and too good. You have no value, but you represent everything that we value.

Rape is a rare non-partisan issue: Democrat/Republican, Congress/BJP, Kuomintang/Communist, Liberal/Reform, Labour/Conservative—no one has a monopoly on either victimhood or culpability.

The US currently has a proud sexual predator at the helm.[75] He has said things so sexist and disgusting that sometimes I read the newspaper and wonder if I'm reading a nasty spoof instead. During the election, as the ugliness escalated, many of us thought with each new revelation or soundbite or tweet that surely now he was done for, but he just wouldn't go away. Plenty of men, and women, thought he was our only hope for the future. And, after the Russians and the Electoral College System each did their bit, there he is in the White House, spewing venom at every turn. For people who have been assaulted, especially by an authority figure, this is devastating. The Big Bad Wolf is in charge and there is nowhere to turn.

In every community, large or small, the person in charge sets the tone. Family culture, school culture, national culture: we look to our leaders to figure out how to think, and what to prioritize. When the president of the country boasts about assaulting women, he might as well be issuing a licence to men that this is an acceptable way to act, and to women that being attacked and dehumanized is their due.

No wonder Sean's patient wept inconsolably.

Marital rape is not considered a crime in thirty-eight countries, including India, where the Research Institute of

Compassionate Economics reports that the vast majority of rapists are the victims' own husbands.[76] In September 2017, the government of India actually spoke out *against* outlawing marital rape. Government lawyers stated that making it a crime would destabilize the institution of marriage, and that we shouldn't blindly follow the West in these matters: husband harassment might become a real problem. We should concentrate instead on things like poverty. The government brief is a masterpiece, with gems like: "What may appear to be marital rape to an individual wife may not appear so to others. As to what constitutes marital rape and what would constitute marital non-rape, it needs to be defined precisely before a view on its criminalization is taken."[77]

It goes on. In India, we have men—and women—at the top saying heinous things about sexual assault, at the same time as hundreds of thousands of people march in the streets calling for better laws. President Duterte in the Philippines joked that an Australian rape victim was so beautiful, the mayor should have had first dibs with her.[78] Grace Mugabe said that mini-skirts invite rape.[79]

In a 2009 AIDS-Free World Report, *Electing to Rape: Sexual Terror in Mugabe's Zimbabwe*,[80] the authors pithily sum up the implications of leaders who, in speech or action, actively promote rape, especially in times of conflict:

> *Tyrants with pathological cravings for power have organized campaigns of rape since ancient times, from Troy to Nanking and Sierra Leone to Cyprus, from East Pakistan to the Democratic Republic of the Congo and beyond. And yet, everyone ever convicted of orchestrating mass rape could be*

> *crowded into a single holding cell ... They know it's*
> *easy to conscript impoverished men and boys raised*
> *in sexist societies to "take charge" of women in*
> *exchange for small pay. They know that deploying*
> *rape brigades is cheap and expeditious: no heavy*
> *weaponry, training, or maneuvers. They know that*
> *targeting women breaks the backbones, the will,*
> *and the cohesion of communities, leaving them*
> *vulnerable. Most crucial, they know that the world*
> *is blind to women ...*

Too many leaders continue to disappoint, but one thing has changed. More than ever, we are *talking* about how our leaders—political, cultural—talk about rape. And that can't be bad. Three decades ago (this is my not-so-random reference point) we might not have made as much of an issue of the fact that the people setting health care policy for American women, the people deciding what services are offered to rape victims or pregnant teenagers, are all white men.

Now that Donald Trump is the leader of the so-called free world, is it good or bad that the most venal side of male behavior is on full display?

Flowers grow in shit. Donald Trump helped fertilize #MeToo. His election, the Women's March, the groundswell of rage that grew out of watching his administration's contempt for anyone but themselves—all this acted as fertilizer for #MeToo. The Weinstein revelations just seemed like the last straw. Women had had enough and were ready to speak at last—at least those who felt they could.

Maybe some good will come of forcing us to confront the grossness we live with every day, including everything from a butt-pinch on the subway to rape and murder behind the curtain of the jungle, with no witnesses but a passing sunbird, flying indifferently on to the next flower.

16

A brief pause for fury

I AM AT A Bat Mitzvah in a serene temple in Cambridge, Massachusetts. Early fall sunshine on the madly mismatched leaves outside, and, inside, a roomful of supportive people, celebrating a young girl's coming of age. The rabbi has long grey hair and one of those wise-woman faces, someone who has seen it all and continues to smile. She welcomes us all joyously. She talks about how we can all work to make the world better each day. She gets us to say "Hallelujah" many times. She is most appropriately uplifting, and her general outlook matches mine, so I am not sure why I'm squirming in my seat and getting increasingly annoyed. Then, just like that, as if a toxic bolt came crashing through the sunlit window and oxidized my mood—I am in a complete rage.

He sent her a rose the next day!

I am remembering how a fellow student raped my friend Hillary, choked her, terrorized her, and then sent her a rose the next day. He moved to North Carolina and might still be there. I am so angry. The rabbi is talking about love and redemption and I am drowning in a sea of bile and bitterness. *He sent her a rose*. I don't want to hear about love and joy and bluebirds singing in the lilacs. I want to:

- Stomp out of the room.
- Get in a car.
- Drive to Interstate 90 West.
- Take Exit 9 for I-84.
- Take Exit 57 for CT-15S.
- Take Exit 86 to merge onto I-91.
- And so on and so forth through 87, 95, 80, 40, I-495, etc. etc.
- (Stop to pee somewhere along the way—my bladder works diligently even in fantasies.)
- Get to NC-540.
- Get Google to tell me exactly where he lives.
- And, twelve hours after leaving the temple…
- Find him.
- Kill him.

Failing that, I want to get up and shout RAPE! The way someone might stand up and shout FIRE! Imagine that—how many of the women in the room would instinctively cross their legs?

The rabbi is not to blame for this choking fury—she is doing her job and doing it well. And I'm not generally a rageful person. It's just that there is a raw ember of anger in me, usually buried under all my perfectly genuine good cheer and faith in humankind, and sometimes it flares up. I wonder if all survivors have it. It's anger at the sheer callousness and carelessness of men who rape. Carelessness about someone else's feelings, carelessness about another human being's integrity. So careless that you would send a rose the next day, maybe not even knowing that what you did was wrong, or that you have now made another person's life so much more difficult—for what? Do you even remember later?

They get away with it and don't give a damn, and I just want to go to North Carolina and commit murder.

17

Rx—polite conversation

The whole system creates the dichotomy between pure women and women to fuck.

—Kalki Koechlin

I GREW UP in a pretty open household. We discussed anything that came up at the dinner table. Rape never came up. Somehow, it just doesn't.

After the December 16th, 2012 gang rape and murder in India, when my old article started to circulate on the internet, I realized that, for all the openness in my own household, I had an eleven-year-old who had no idea about this part of my past. It had never come up. Somehow, it just doesn't.

The eleven-year-old did know what rape is. She just didn't know it had happened to me. Somehow the moment had never been right. And now the moment had come, to tell her before she heard about it from someone else.

What to say? How to present it? Would she be trauma-tized? She was such a dear little thing, and I was her tough *Amma*. How on earth was I going to tell her that this terrible thing had happened to me? I lost sleep. I called people. I agonized. Until the other parent, my wise partner, put it all into perspective.

"I think you're forgetting something really important," he said. "All this craziness around rape, all the baggage, is our baggage. She doesn't have any. She doesn't know it's supposed to be shameful or destroy you or any of those things. She just knows you. She sees you're strong and happy. That's what matters."

One of my smarter moves was marrying this man.

The Big Moment happened at breakfast, not dinner. I just said it. Since she already knew about sexual violence, I didn't have to go into that whole song and dance. I said, it happened to me when I was seventeen, some men raped me, I was hurt, everybody took care of me, and I'm fine now. Then I shut up and waited for her to freak out, be horrified, judge me, weep, wail, lose faith in the world.

She heard me, took it in, and said, "Okay. Can you please pass the cheese?" And that was that. Now it's just another part of our family story.

I hope she never has to deal with this issue. But I'm sure she will. We must face the fact—no matter how glorious a life she has, at some point someone in it will be raped. And, when that happens, she will know that it is possible to survive and flourish, and she will know that it is not the first time. These things sound so small and simple, but they are everything. Ask anyone who has ever felt alone and hopeless.

When the piece came out, my brother called me at six in the morning (I was in bed with the covers over my head, kicking myself for being such a total idiot and exposing myself this way, and refusing to look at the paper). He had to tell his twelve-year-old son before school, as they read the *Times* in class every day and he was going to see his aunt all over the editorial page. So my brother told him, and got the same calm interested-in-a-vague-kind-of-way response. And that, once again, was that.

It's so easy! It's so easy to just tell them. We talk with them about genocides and justice, dying planets and those who murder them, corruption and chaos, but somehow sexual violence sends us into a tailspin of uncertainty and general mush-for-brains incoherence. Let's just stop that. It's so much easier now than it was even five years ago, now that it really has become much more part of the conversation.

Manassah Bradley was a happy-go-lucky teenage boy at a Boston high school for high-achieving students. One day a teacher he didn't know asked him to come into the book room to help stack books. Manassah told me his story.

"We went into the room and it quickly turned into a rape and attempted murder. He had his hands around my neck while he was raping me and I thought he was going to kill me. It was really bad. I blacked out and went to another place. I was floating above myself. It was beautiful. Then I thought, if you don't fight back, you're going to die. I started fighting. After it was over, I went to the school nurse and said I was sick, and they just let me go home. I was in shock, catatonic. It was as if I was walking through a picture that was painted by Dalí or Picasso. I was in a totally surreal place. I went home, thinking, you just have to pull yourself together. I got home. My mother said, 'What happened? Are you okay?'

"I said nothing, because I didn't know what happened. I didn't know what rape was so I couldn't say, 'Mom, I was raped today.' A year and a half later, my aunts were talking about Connie Francis, how she was raped at gunpoint. I heard them and thought, that's what happened to me!"

He didn't know what rape was, and so he couldn't tell anyone. Unfortunately, his ordeal wasn't over. Years later, when he called a rape crisis center, they hung up on him after saying that men could not be raped; they could only be rapists. (This would not happen now, decades later.) When he went to the police, they said nobody would believe his word against the teacher's, and he should go home and forget about it.

In 2013, Bishop Desmond Tutu, Jacob Lief (founder and CEO of Ubuntu Pathways) and I wrote a joint piece in *The Guardian*,[81] in which we said:

> *Rape has become a ubiquitous global topic, and that is encouraging since it is a global blot on our collective humanity. But hardly anyone has paid attention to how this affects the most important group of all: the next generation, which is poised to inherit our poisonous baggage.*
>
> *… The three of us deal with this issue in different ways every day of our lives, yet we too are guilty of protesting articulately outside but leaving it on the other side of the door when we sit down to dinner with our families. Until rape, and the structures— sexism, inequality, tradition—that make it possible are part of our dinner table conversation with the next generation, it will continue. Is it polite and comfortable to talk about it? No. Must we anyway? Yes.*

... You do not lose innocence when you learn about terrible acts; you lose your innocence when you commit them. An open culture of tolerance, honesty, and discussion is the best way to safeguard innocence, not destroy it.

The house I grew up in was on a lovely country lane. We had a winding driveway from the house to the gate, and when my brother and I were small we spent hours, years, playing by ourselves in the garden. Occasionally we would walk to the gate to look out at the world. One afternoon, a man walked by and beckoned us closer. We went, and he pulled out his penis, waved it at us, and went on his way. We were a bit bewildered by this, but not particularly traumatized. We didn't tell anybody.

Why not? We weren't ashamed. We weren't hurt or frightened, but it was certainly an odd event and we told our parents about other odd events. But we never told, and life went on.

I don't consider this penis-waving particularly heinous, although of course it comes under the rubric of sexual abuse of some kind or other. My point is that we had no framework or language to talk or think about it. I wonder whether, if he had come in and actually tried to touch one of us, we would have fled, told someone, or just stood there mesmerized. The whole thing faded from memory, and my only regret now is that we never had the gratification of watching our mother give the guy the yelling of his life.

I asked a friend if he has talked about sexual abuse with his nine-year-old daughter. His reply was, "What I have told her is, being naked at home with your family is okay; being naked with strangers is not, and if someone says they want to be naked with you who is not Papa or Daddy you need to tell us right away. If we are not available, find an old lady nearby and ask her for help."

Imagine if someone had talked about this with eighty-four-year-old Dulcie, who was raped by multiple people as a child when she was growing up in the Great Depression. Imagine if someone had taken the trouble to explain the basic mechanics of human reproduction to her, and she had not suffered agonies for years after being raped, terrified every month that she might be pregnant.

Even if telling our children about rape is relatively simple, talking to them about rape culture is much more complicated.

A friend told me about reading Osamu Tezuka's *Buddha* graphic novels with her nine-year-old brother. "He asked me, 'Why are the women naked?'" she said. She told him to look more closely. She said, "They are topless just like the men, not naked." In his mind, men could expose their chests and remain dressed, but women had to be fully covered. He had no idea that it was possible to have the same standards for both. It's a small thing, but these are the conversations we need to have.

If you need evidence of double standards, you can find plenty in the unsavoury dynamics in many households—the ones where the dear little boy is his mummy's *ladla*, little darling, and is used to being served and getting whatever he wants, chop chop. These little boys might grow into men who are fond of their mothers, but that doesn't necessarily translate into respect for women like their wives or every other female on the planet. It's more a kind of appreciation that there's a whole world of worshipful slaves-with-sexy-parts out there.

Long ago, I lived in a rooftop apartment in Delhi. My landlady lived below with her teenage son and daughter. Our local ironing lady, Rampyari, set up shop under a nearby tree. I can still see her at her table with her giant iron. She heated it by filling it with glowing coals, supplied from a nearby fire tended by her ancient husband. When the landlady's daughter had clothes to iron, she would walk over and hand them to Rampyari. When the son wanted his shirts done, he just opened his window and flung them out to her. If they landed in the dust, she was responsible for cleaning them off. Every time I saw him yelling out the window and then throwing his clothes at her, watching to see if she caught them in time, I went into a solitary rage and stomped around my terrace muttering to myself.

Rape culture. The totality of all the big and little things we do, say and believe that ultimately lead to the conclusion that it's okay to rape. Perhaps not any one of the little things: serving your son first like a good Indian mother doesn't mean you condone rape; making fun of lady drivers doesn't mean you condone rape; saving for your daughter's dowry doesn't mean you condone rape; saying "boys will be boys" on the playground doesn't mean you condone rape. But each of these chips away at women's and girls' self-respect, and gives boys permission to feel a little more entitled, a little more important, a little more as though they have a free pass to maraud through the world and take without thinking.

If we want to teach our children to be decent human beings who respect others and themselves, we have to tackle notions of masculinity and femininity. And patriarchy. No, don't run away. We really do.

Feminist writer, theorist and professor Cynthia Enloe writes: [82]

> *Patriarchy is a particular complex web of both attitudes and relationships that position women and men, girls and boys in distinct and unequal categories, that value particular forms of masculinity over virtually all forms of femininity, and—and this is crucial—that ensure that men who fulfill these favored forms of manliness will be able to assert control over most women.*
>
> *In other words, patriarchy is wide and it is deep. It is distinct, but it feeds off both racism and classism.*
>
> *Patriarchy's workings are not automatically rejected by women and girls. There are many rewards bestowed on a woman who finds ways to fit into a patriarchal system: marital economic security, societal respectability; even, occasionally, state honors. The woman who does not rebel against patriarchy will be complimented on her beauty, on her femininity, on her loyalty (as a daughter, a wife, a secretary); she will be praised for her endurance, her good sense, her domestic skills, her maternal devotion, her sexual appeal, her caring sacrifice.*

We can't talk about male privilege without talking about the women who also benefit from that by playing along. And these are the conversations we must have within our families: the rewards and drawbacks of going along with a system that says men take and women let them.

In his therapy groups of 11th and 12th-graders (16–18 years old), New York counselor Sean Grover often asks the participants to consider a hypothetical situation. Imagine two kids your age, a boy and a girl, who like each other and decide to have sex. It's going to be the first time for both of them. They are both excited about it and spend a lot of energy planning, discussing, arranging the perfect situation. Finally they're in it, privacy, condoms, everything taken care of. They start making out and undressing. Suddenly the girl says, "I've changed my mind. I don't want to do this any more." What should happen?

There's invariably a split in the group, Sean told me. It's not predictable—the boys and girls aren't always on the same side. But there's always an argument between those who believe that she has a right to say no at any point and stop, and those who say, "That's not fair! They decided. She can't stop now."

These are not soldiers ordered by their commander to rape women in refugee camps, or men in masks hiding behind the bushes waiting for a likely target to jog by. They are privileged twenty-first-century American adolescents whose parents have the means to send them to therapy to talk about their feelings. These boys could grow up to be Brock Turner, or to be the men who came to the aid of the woman he sexually assaulted.

These conversations are about more than yes and no. They get to the heart of what it means to be a man, and our take on masculinity and femininity.

Dismissal at my daughter's school on a sunny early-fall day. A mixed group of teenagers of all shapes, sizes and races are talking on the curb. I glance cursorily over at them: the brown guy in the hoodie, the black girl in leggings, the six-foot blond boy in a cute little red dress that shows off his hairy legs. I do a double-take and resist the urge to grin at him and give him a thumbs-up, afraid of being patronizing.

Is he bi, trans, he, she, they? Is he just feeling pretty today? Why would he care that a random woman approves of him? Nobody else seems the least bit concerned.

This is fabulous. When we start to subvert our traditional ideas of what it means to be manly or womanly, when an unshaven teenager wears a dress to school and it isn't a big deal, we are getting to the heart of all our assumptions about power, agency and entitlement. And there's a direct line from there to how we treat people, and to the conditions that could finally make rape an aberration instead of just another everyday occurrence.

In 2012, sexual assailants contributed their side of the story for a Reddit post and I quote here verbatim what they wrote.[83] One wrote:

> *I was a freshman and hooking up with this girl who got naked in bed with me, then said no. I think she just wanted to do oral. I was extremely horny and already close to doing it, so I ignored her and did it. She realized what was happening and tried to clamp her legs shut, but it was too late and I was much stronger than her.*

Another wrote:

> *I'm a good-looking guy, and I can get girls pretty easily. I'm currently married to a beautiful woman that I met during this time of my life (not someone I raped, but someone who knew my mask during this time). So, anyways, after a while it became boring to go after the sluts and sorority girls that would easily throw their cunt after you. I wanted the thrill of the chase, and*

that's what led me to forcing myself on girls. I would find attractive girls that were self-conscious about their looks. Girls who were pretty in their own unique way, but not the outgoing sort, mostly introverts, and girls that didn't party or do wild things. Hopefully a girl who was a bit damaged, had a shitty ex-boyfriend, or family issues, came from a small shut-in town, that sort of thing. So, when I showed interest in them they'd be completely enamored, they'd almost be shocked that a popular, good-looking, and well liked guy would be talking to them. I'd have that initial meeting at the library, a coffee shop, a work function, or a party, where I had them convinced of what a great guy I was. I listened to them, and made them feel special, like they were a princess. Sometimes we might sort of hook-up that night (kissing, making-out, never anything more). The next day I'd call, and see when they wanted to get together again. I'd feign some excuse for not going out somewhere, but having them come over late in the night. It was college, and not a lot of people had transportation off campus, so it was typical for people to come over and watch a movie or something on a date.

They would come over, and I'd always make sure it was real cold in the room, cold enough so that when we started watching the movie I'd say something about being chilly, and grab a big fleece blanket for the both of us. We'd get kind of close, and then maybe ignore the movie for some kissing. After a while, we'd talk some more, and I'd start edging my hands around the under strap of the bra, or maybe a bit into her pants, just kind of playing on the edge to gauge her response. Some girls would stiffen up a little, and that's when you knew they didn't like what was going on. We were in my studio apartment, so the bed served as the couch, and it was easy to start sliding down throughout the movie so we'd be laying down. It was then that I could turn around and get on top of her. The girls usually didn't know how to respond. Some of them were into it, and those nights were usually consensual and boring sex, sometimes followed up by a few more nightly visits before getting the boot. However, the great nights were the ones who squirmed, ones who didn't want to give in. I'd have to shush them down, and try to work on them slowly enough so they didn't know what was going on until it was pretty much already happening. I'm a muscular guy, over 6' around 200 lbs. and most of these girls may have been 125–130, really tiny and easy to pin down. To be honest, even remembering it now, the squirming always made it better, they didn't want it to happen, but they couldn't do anything about it. Most girls don't say no either. They think you're a good guy, and should pick up on the hints, they don't want to have to say "no" and admit to themselves what's happening. Alcohol helped. Having a few drinks during the movie, or doing a few jello shots that were "prepared for a party that weekend" would usually do the trick.

The aftermath was always different. Some girls left about 15 minutes after. Some girls would stay until the morning and then leave. A few tried to call back, maybe blaming themselves for what happened or something. I never worried too much about being caught. Everyone knew me, and I worked with the police a lot, with administrators, and campus officials. I was on first-name basis with the Chancellor and the President of Student Affairs, so if anything came down to a he/she-said I figured I'd be in the clear. Having her come over to my place also made it seem less predatory, as she came into my domain, and "could leave at any time".

Reading these accounts reminds me why it is dangerous when we say that rape has nothing to do with sex. The way we talk about sex absolutely feeds into rape culture. Talking to children about consent and agency as soon as you can talk to them at all is so important. Nicole Cushman, from Answer, a sex education organization, explains it perfectly:[84]

High-quality sex education can and should equip young people with the language and tools to understand and critique the roles of gender and power in their friendships and romantic relationships. Creating safe classroom spaces for students to explore these topics can begin to create cultural shifts in gender norms and related behaviors… Only by openly addressing these issues and laying bare the discrepancies and dissonance that underlie rape culture can we begin to create a new paradigm in which victims are believed, boundaries are respected, and healthy relationships are established.

Life would be healthier all around if women spent less time being frightened and more being righteously indignant. Why are we so afraid of "angry women"? I think we owe it to our daughters to teach them that some things are really worth getting angry about.

Laila Atshan, the Palestinian social worker, told me about a recent workshop with "twenty ladies in a room." They were worried about their children being abused, in the midst of the tense atmosphere of the Occupied Territories. They were reluctant to talk to their daughters and add more fear to their already tense lives. She told them, "Don't hush-hush. Problems like ants become elephants if you ignore them and don't deal with them."

Excellent advice, although rape is neither an ant or an elephant—let's leave the animal kingdom out of it. As I've said before, words are powerful. If a child has been molested, she or he is much less likely to report it if she doesn't know what words to use.

Children are generally clever little sponges, adept at picking up cues. So talking to them about respect and consent is important but not enough. We must model it, which is a constant challenge. Maybe other people are more enlightened than me, but I know that, no matter how savvy I think I am, I can so easily slip into making sexist/racist/ cultural assumptions. Why did I feel so delighted when I saw a young woman in a hijab reading Sylvia Plath in an airport lounge? Why the hell *wouldn't* she read Sylvia Plath? My approval was every bit as patronizing as my father's colleagues patting me on the head when I got good report cards in school.

The notion of honor is a tricky one too. In much of the world, rape dishonors a woman, her family, and her community. In places like the US, despite the current moment of catharsis, raped women are still too often seen as spoiled goods, by themselves as well as others. This is a huge burden to carry. I've written about how rape should not be associated with honor. But there's another way to look at it. Why don't we flip the "honor" label around, and put it where it belongs?

In 2013, Sami Faltas, a father of three daughters from the Netherlands, wrote this to me:

> *It is a matter of honour for men to fight crimes, of whatever nature, against women. It is a matter of honour for men to treat women with the respect they deserve. Let's not take honour out of the equation, but redefine it.*

Sounds eminently sensible and righteous to me.

18

All in the family

He kept telling me he was my uncle, and I must respect him.

—Nomawethu, raped when she was five years old

NOMAWETHU'S family lived in Grahamstown, in a rural part of South Africa. Her father's brother raped her when she was five. Everyone knew what happened: "They saw blood in my panties. And on his T-shirt," she told me.

Her father wanted to kill him. Her mother wanted to report him, but at a family meeting it was decided not to do that, and her mother couldn't defy the decision as she was afraid of her husband. "My father was physically abusive to my mother," Nomawethu told me. When her mother could, she fled to her own family, leaving Nomawethu behind. As soon as she could, she came back and fetched her. They moved far away, and Nomawethu grew up, went to school, and passed her exams. She had no memory of the rape and no idea that anything had happened. "I was able to block it," she told me.

In 2002, after she matriculated, Nomawethu's mother told her, "You are a grown-up young lady now, you can reunite with your father," and Nomawethu traveled back to her native village to see her father for the first time in thirteen years. There, she met her uncle, and the rape memory reared up like a wild beast and completely overwhelmed her. "I had no idea anything had happened, and it all came back in detail." She asked her mother about it as soon as she got home. Her mother corroborated everything, and Nomawethu had to figure out how to integrate the sudden onslaught of painful memory and information.

"Seeing him now, I feel nothing but pity. I just feel sad for him. For a grown-up to do that to a little child..." She did her best to put everything behind her, figuring that she had managed fine before she remembered. But it's never simple with rape, and incest can be even more complicated and insidious.

Nomawethu manages the early childhood program at Ubuntu Pathways in Port Elizabeth, South Africa. I met her there when I was working at Ubuntu and writing for them. It's a unique place—it caters to some of the most disenfranchized people on earth, each one with a story to break your heart, but it is a happy place of strength and song. Nomawethu fits right in.

Despite her fulfilling life and job, she started to have panic attacks at work. "It's catching up," she realized. "I haven't dealt with it." She is seeing a psychologist to help her come to terms with her past, and making progress. But it's not easy.

How do you trust, when the basic unit of trust—the family—is corroded?

"I met my husband. He is very loving to me, very supportive. As much as I trust him, when it comes to my daughter (six years old), I can't even trust him as the father," Nomawethu said. She hates this, hates the unfair suspicions and hair-trigger reactions that so many survivors must contend with. For example, her daughter had worms at one point—a common, minor childhood occurrence. "But, when she complained that her private parts hurt, I freaked out." Her brain immediately jumped to thoughts of sexual abuse. "I don't want to be like that."

So many children, so many uncles, fathers, cousins … one South African woman was raped by her brother when she was very young, and did not tell anyone until she was well into middle age. Her family must have known something was going on, especially when she acquired a sexually transmitted infection, but people are amazingly skilled at pretending everything is normal when it is not. As soon as this woman told her children about her history, she went into a deep depression from which she never fully recovered.

I've written earlier about Angie, who was raped by her husband. As with so many other people, this was not the only abusive relationship in her life. She told me that, when she was a child and living briefly in South India, her family's driver would take her out in the car and touch her. Oh, and of course there was also the inappropriate uncle or two.

She grew up privileged, in a happy family. Mostly happy, anyway. There was the driver and the uncles, but this is not unusual, and it isn't the main part of her story. She had a love marriage, meaning that her Indian family didn't arrange it. She and her husband met, fell in love, and got married. He was a charming and successful man, and her family was thrilled. The couple moved to the US right away, and Angie, very much in love, couldn't wait to have babies. She had four miscarriages and then two children, who are now in college and high school. "If not for them, I would have lost my will to live."

The abuse started slowly, as these things tend to do—a harsh word here, a slap there, then remorse. It began during her second pregnancy.

Angie felt keenly that she had nobody to blame but herself, since she had opted for a love marriage rather than an arranged one. She kept it to herself, and told her sister when she had to—her sister had to drive her, injured and pregnant, to the hospital. The sister reacted with fury, accused her of lying, and simultaneously told her she'd better shut up and bear it.

And bear it she did, for far too long. "Don't get me wrong. There were moments when I did not want to live," she told me. "It took me a little time to understand it. He would hit me. And then say, said, '*Tum ne khud se kar liya* (you did this to yourself).'"

After the abuse was well and truly established and she faced the reality of her situation, she felt unable to leave because of her immigration status. "He said the day I left, he would send me back to India and I would never see my children again."

She started talking to lawyers to try to figure out how she could leave her husband without losing her children. Every step of the way was difficult in every way. For one thing, she is a deeply religious Muslim, which gave her strength but also caused her to question herself. "Allah gave me strength," she told me proudly. On the other hand, she was very conscious of her duty as a wife and the spectre of bringing shame to the family.

"What makes you stay is hope," she told me. "And what makes you leave is hope, that things could get better."

Her home life became a constant drama. Her husband hired private detectives to follow her. His behavior was erratic.

"There's so much confusion when you're going through it," Angie said. "You have a peaceful thought sometimes, but this was so confusing. This person said he loved me, but he behaved differently with me when we were alone. I was in a fog.

"He is very suave and polite and charming and makes a lot of money. People said, 'You have everything.' They had no idea what I was going through.

"It's hard to understand. People say, 'Why didn't you just leave?' It's not so easy. This person has power over you."

On her younger son's ninth birthday, her husband got upset that he couldn't find something. "He took out all my clothes and told my younger son to throw them all away. One of his friends called his mother, who called the police. He took our son out and started to play ball. When the police came, he said, 'I don't know what's going on.' The police officer came in and he knew me from my volunteer work. I told him what happened, and showed him. He said, 'Get the kids together.' He spoke to my husband and then I got in the car with my children and drove away. That was one incident.

"We had so much property. He ruined everything. Everything was in foreclosure. I was devastated in every way."

Ultimately, he filed for divorce. He accused her of abusing their sons and wanted full custody.

Her aunt called her shameless. Her husband called her a whore. Her brother wanted to know if she had cheated. But she persevered, and, after a long court battle in the US, she won full custody of her children.

How did she have the strength? I wanted to know.

"It's Allah. I performed Hajj in 1995. My faith, my family, and my sons saved me."

She still insists her sons visit their father, although they don't like doing it. "As a Muslim woman, *apna farz hai*. I must do my duty."

Nomawethu, Angie, many, many of my own friends and acquaintances—I am reminded over and over that rape is not just the monster *out there*—it's the monster under the bed of our childhood nightmares. It leaves ugly wounds, and sometimes we have to make a new, safer family to provide the haven that "home" never was, and to heal the wounds of both body and spirit.

19

A brief pause for confusion

IN THE FALL of 2017, the international news was suddenly full of women who were abused and terrorized by men, who stayed in relationships (personal, professional) with their abusers and have said they had conflicting feelings. This may sound confusing, and I've had friends express doubts to me about how severely these women were really victimized. Maybe it wasn't so bad?

No, no, no. This is a tough one to grasp, I know, so I repeat: no, no, no. How you act with your rapist afterwards, and even how you might *feel* about your rapist afterwards, doesn't indicate the seriousness of either the crime or your trauma.

In the midst of my own shock and pain all those years ago, I felt a fugitive pang for the people who raped me. I had no history with them. They were strangers full of hostility and rage and I had nothing in common with them. I looked into their eyes and felt sick with panic. But I also felt a weird compassion.

I think calling it Stockholm Syndrome and labeling it a pathology or a dysfunctional response is too simplistic. I didn't like them, or sympathize, or understand. But I did see that in some odd way they were fellow human beings. And they were not happy. They were not having a fine old time, out for a jolly gang-bang. Maybe some men have fun committing rape, but these men weren't. It was all terrifying for me, but they were also tormented, and I couldn't help noticing that and feeling a tiny chord of empathy.

Oddly enough, this might have been what saved my life that day. Their plan was to kill us, my friend and me. I talked and talked and talked—I've never talked that much before or since. I forgot that I was supposed to be a shy kid. I talked about how I knew they were good people, we were all brothers and sisters, blah blah…

Let me be very clear, I did *not* think they were good people or that we were brothers and sisters. I thought, and still do, that they were extremely bad people. They were malign, brutal, and vicious. But it was the only way I could think of to get them to see me as someone they couldn't destroy. Or themselves as people who couldn't kill. And perhaps the only way I could do that was to believe it a tiny bit myself.

If the world were different and I had seen them in court, would I have felt sorry for them? I have no idea. I'm just pointing out that it makes perfect sense to me when I see photographs of famous women smiling and hugging men whom they later point out as rapists. The fact that you have confused feelings about the person who hurt you doesn't make you guilty. It makes you human.

20

Stealing freedom, stealing joy

It took from me. Something was taken from me.

—Alexa

Leave your pain here, and go out and do your magnificent things.

—Judge Rosemarie Aquilina, 30th Circuit Court,
Ingham County, Michigan, to one of the
victims of serial abuser Larry Nassar

IF I REJECT the notion of rape taking away women's "honor" —and I do—then what does it take from you?

I think much of it has to do with your right to joy. How do you, the victim, hold on to a sense of joy, that fragile thing, as you continue with your life afterwards? Rape is just one of the many things that can rob you of that—is it special in some way, requiring special intervention to let the light back in?

Much has been written about the loss of control that goes with sexual assault. Loss of control is painful and difficult no matter how it happens, and with rape it can be particularly fraught. How do you get that control back?

This also plays into the question of how a society/family/individual views sex. Is sex meant for pleasure or procreation? This matters deeply because it influences the way we talk to young people about their relationship to sex, and their bodies. It also influences the recovery process.

Alexa is a Puerto Rican New Yorker. I liked her on sight—she is brave and energetic and totally committed to getting through the pain of being raped twice within five months.

"I grew up very sex-positive," she told me. Her aunt worked in a reproductive health agency, and gave her plenty of information and advice. "I was always very informed. I had very good sexual experiences until this occurred."

"This" occurred when she was a junior in college. She was dating a fellow student, an older man who was a veteran of the US war in Iraq. The relationship soured quickly.

"He was weird. I wanted out. On his birthday night, we were in a bar. He was drunk. Mean. I went to the restroom and cried. When I came out, I told him I was done, and started to walk out. He screamed at me, 'You fucking whore!' I was at the door. I stopped and turned around and said, 'Thank you, you just made it easier.'"

She went to another bar with some people she knew. She was shaken up but pleased to have said what she said. Someone offered her a Xanax, which she'd never taken before. She took it, had some drinks, and then had some more drinks.

"I sort of browned-out." She knew, tripping over herself on her way back to the dorm, that she had overdone it. She went to bed. He came over and knocked on her door. She opened it and told him he should leave. She was unsteady on her feet.

"He pushed his way in. He was huge. Tall. Heavy. I wobbled."

He pushed her onto the bed. She passed out, and woke up with him on top. She said, "Get off!" He said, "You're finished when I say you're finished." She was so frightened that she complied. He raped her and left.

"It felt so surreal," she reported to me. "I wanted to press charges. I knew I had no case. I let it go. I didn't tell my family." She told a friend, who skeptically asked, "Are you sure?" A few weeks later, she went to a gynaecologist and asked to be checked for sexually transmitted infections. She told the doctor that she was concerned because her boyfriend had been cheating on her, with sex workers. The doctor said, "Maybe you should have been saving it for marriage."

"How did I find so much judgment? In New York!"

Alexa soon found out that the rapist, who was a resident advisor at the college, had raped other girls as well, and spread stories about them. She felt helpless to do anything, but she felt increasingly guilty, as if it was her fault that he was still at large. In the months that followed, he became a federal air marshal.

She continued to go about her business, but she felt different. "I doubted everything about myself." Her grades dropped. "The worst part had to be—I became distant. Not myself."

Just when she was feeling the most rattled, someone introduced her to cocaine "at absolutely the wrong time."

She quickly got hooked. Her mother noticed that she seemed different, and asked her what was wrong. Alexa told her. It was against her better judgement, but she had received no support from anyone, and was feeling desperate.

"My mom said, 'What did you think was going to happen?' That led to a full unraveling."

A few months later, she found an internship on Wall Street, working for an abusive man. They were attracted to each other, and she fell into a dysfunctional atmosphere of abuse by multiple men, and "non-stop drugs and drinking at work." The boss had sex with her when she was drunk or high, and invited other people to watch. She was raped again. Finally, he fired her.

"I fell apart."

She became "a shell of a person." She had no friends, and didn't graduate on time. Her mother found some cocaine in her room and disowned her.

Feeling she had to do it alone, Alexa was determined to get her spirit back. She tried to distract herself. She helped in the clean-up efforts after Hurricane Katrina. She had her breasts reduced. She went to South Africa to study. She relied on alcohol and cocaine to keep her going.

"I would go out but I always had an awful time. I see it in pictures—the spark gone from my eyes."

So how did she get the spark back?

"It took so much," she said. "It took me not killing myself." She was suicidal for a long time. She only didn't do it because "I didn't want someone to find me."

"I felt like I was not a person."

This went on for eight years. She couldn't have an orgasm. She couldn't feel happy. "I felt very broken. I stopped dating." She thought she would try the church. "I told a priest that I had a dire need to speak. He said, 'I have plans,' and asked me to come back between nine and five on a weekday. That's when I lost faith in the Church." She thought it would never end. "No one was there for me."

She went to a psychiatrist, who told her she was bipolar and gave her meds, which she didn't take. She exercised instead, and felt better. She didn't give up. "What got me through was hope."

The healing was incremental. It started with one person. Her childhood best friend heard she wasn't doing well and reached out to her. Then she found a therapy group, where she told her story and felt very supported. She exercises regularly, remains sober, and is in a happy relationship.

She recently googled the rapist. He is registered at Babies R Us with his wife. They are going to have a little girl.

"They go about their lives," she said bitterly. "They put poison in the water and we have to drain it out."

One therapist told me about a woman client who told him stories that seemed somehow incomplete, like accounts of being blackout drunk that she couldn't fully explain, even to herself. One day, she went for a massage and suddenly started having flashbacks. Bit by bit she realized that she had been raped by three of her brother's friends.

"After she realized what had happened to her, she changed completely," he told me. "She started to recover her boundaries."

Boundaries. It's such a first-world word, but it really is useful. In India, the only boundaries we (only occasionally) agree on are physical ones between our plots of land. Psychologically, it's a free-for-all and might is right. Whoever has power in the family, community, country gets to trample all over everyone else's boundaries.

When I became a rape crisis counselor, I had to learn about boundaries. Here is how the organization Mothers of Sexually Abused Children (MOSAC) defines them:[85]

> *A boundary is similar to a border, a place where you stop and the other person starts. When boundaries are invaded, a person has entered territory belonging to the other person. This may be an emotional boundary, a physical boundary, or a sexual boundary. Boundaries also exist in other areas, however. Telling someone how to think violates their mental boundaries. Telling them how to spend their money violates their financial boundaries. Abuses are usually identified by the boundaries that have been violated (e.g. physical abuse, sexual abuse, mental abuse, emotional abuse).*
>
> *Sexual abuse violates almost all conceivable boundaries of a human being. The lines are crossed physically, sexually, emotionally, mentally, and spiritually. This violation leaves the victim in a boundary-less state. Consequently, the ability to set and maintain future boundaries has been compromised. As an adult, the sexual abuse victim may struggle with boundaries in all relationships.*

I understand this, and have heard many stories from rape survivors about how they had difficulty saying no or getting into healthy relationships. It can kill sex. Oh, boy, it can. Being raped at a very young age is an effective recipe for terribly confused feelings about sex. Sex can become scary or dirty or just plain joyless. Or, constrained by fear and confusion, you don't have the space to develop sexually.

It blurs boundaries—or it can clarify them. Although I paid for my rape in many other ways, it actually helped me draw very clear boundaries, and for that I've always been grateful. Not to the rapists, of course, but just to whatever contrarian gene I have that hates being told what to do. Perhaps this would have happened anyway. I was so young when I was raped that it's impossible to tease out how much of who I became is because of it. Whatever the reason, I've always felt very clear about how sex is supposed to feel, and how it's *not* supposed to feel, and had no qualms about saying an emphatic *no* to anybody who made me feel even a thousandth of a percent of the way I felt up on the mountain—feeling I don't have a choice, that someone else knows better, that I owe any man anything. Ha! Take that, you person who got all pouty when I didn't appreciate your nipple-clamp schemes. You know who you are.

Another life-sapping result of rape is the huge output of energy it takes to keep secrets. Secrets are like cancer. They mutate in unpredictable ways and create strange distortions. And they have toxic side effects. I read a moving description by an anonymous woman[86] who had two secrets: violent abuse (she does not specify whether it was sexual, but it was certainly brutal and misogynist) by her father; and her own lesbianism. She writes, "And my shame is the biggest way in which my PTSD and lesbianism are linked." Until she shared both secrets, they somehow got intertwined, so that the horror of abuse and the joy of sexual awakening became poisonously combined.

Dulcie is eighty-four years old. She lives in an assisted-living facility with her husband. It's been a long journey to this place. Born in the US in 1933, she is a child of the Great Depression, and a survivor of multiple sexual assaults when she was very young. "My mother used to leave me alone in the apartment house. There was a delivery boy from the store. He used to take me into this apartment—Eileen's apartment, I still remember. He took off my pants, and I don't remember the rest."

That was just the beginning. "The Metropolitan Life insurance man used to meet me on the stairs and make me take my clothes off. Another neighborhood boy made me take my clothes off. I just went with everybody who wanted me."

Dulcie got her first period when she was ten years old. One day she was listening to girls playing outside, and heard them say that you could have a baby if a man did certain things with his penis, and she freaked out.

"I heard this and went into shock and thought I was pregnant. What happened from there was, every month when I was waiting for my period, I worried because I had done all those terrible things. I had been with the insurance man, another man, the high school boy, the boy down the block. I just didn't know what to do. Every month I'd wait to bleed. I was so scared. I didn't tell anyone.

"After that, every time I was friendly with someone or I went out with a boy, until I found out the facts of life, I would go running in the bathroom to check if I had my period."

Finally one day she couldn't bear it and said to her cousin and close friend Grace, "Grace, I'm going to have a baby."

"She said, 'What?!' I said, 'I had men touching me, and I let them.' She took my pants down and looked to see if I was bleeding. I wasn't. She said I didn't do anything wrong. She explained to me that I had been abused. I had been frightened and scared and ashamed. Every day I would wait for my period. It affected my learning, my interaction with people. I was afraid that no one would like me. I was so ashamed of myself.

"I feel that I would have been something more. I would have achieved more. But I couldn't. I felt like a bum. I felt like a dirty outcast."

Feeling dirty, used-up, useless, broken—it's such a part of survivors' lives. One day I got an email from a stranger: "I'm all broken inside, not able to gather myself... broken into pieces... "

Even when rape leaves you your life, it can take you down dangerous paths. The Vera Institute of Justice conducted a study of women prisoners and found that eighty-six percent had a history of sexual abuse.[87] Imagine coming to prison with that in your background, and then coming face-to-face with a new brutal statistic: while women make up thirteen percent of the jailed population, they represent sixty-seven percent of the victims of sexual violence by prison staff. And that's just women: male-on-male rape in prison is, shamefully, the subject of jokes and winks in popular US culture, and I can't imagine the terrible ripple effects that has on individuals, families, and communities.

Just to make sure to sprinkle at least a modicum of insult on top of injury, if your life doesn't get completely decimated or derailed, you can count on some non-life-threatening but highly inconvenient side effects of rape. Trauma literature abounds with descriptions of flashbacks and triggers. "Triggers" is a terrifying word, and rightly so—war veterans are familiar with the phenomenon. But triggers can also be just pains in the ass, a constant eye-rolling bore to deal with. Ask any survivor.

My family had moved to Boston a couple of years before I was raped. Boston is very cold. When you've grown up in

Bombay, it's even colder. Imagine how inconvenient it was, therefore, to be completely unable to wear a scarf around my neck for years. The rapists choked me quite hard, and for a very long time anything in the vicinity of my throat sent me into a tailspin of fright. Friends who came up from behind and put friendly hands on my neck or shoulder would be treated to a total breakdown. After some time, the flashbacks morphed into just an inability to be comfortable with anything tight around my neck. Turtlenecks—brrrr. When that happens, you don't even have the dignity and drama of your history—you just have a Pavlovian response to a stimulus without even thinking about why. It's damn aggravating. I'm so pleased with my giant scarf collection now, and my neck stays nicely wrapped in the New York winters.

One woman I know contracted a sexually transmitted disease from being raped as a child. At that time, she was told she got it from a toilet seat. Although she knows now that she can't possibly contract an STD from a toilet seat, she simply cannot use a public toilet without putting layers of paper on it first, and even after doing that she is uncomfortable for hours.

Another developed just enough of an obsessive-compulsive tic to prevent her from being able to relax and read or watch TV when she was alone at home. She just had to get up and keep checking to make sure she had locked the front door, even though she knew she had already checked ten minutes ago, and ten minutes before that, and ten minutes before that... She finally broke the habit by writing herself notes: *I checked at 5.50. It was correctly locked. I double-checked and made sure!*

Another has to have the lights on during sex. Another freaks out when she sees trousers of a certain color. And too many of us know that sinking feeling every year when we can't help noticing that another macabre anniversary is approaching.

This is not dramatic. It's just tedious and energy-sapping. Reading about things like the "Cognitive Triad of Traumatic Stress" makes it seem like trauma is always highly colored. But sometimes the reality is closer to the opposite: a draining of color, a detraction from living fully, and an enslavement to weird patterns.

I've written earlier about Rida and her sister, who were both assaulted by the same man when they were children, and didn't know this about each other until they were adults. Rida has clear memories: "I remember everything. The color of my pyjamas, when and how I kicked him. It was life altering. I think about it all the time. Every damn day ... "

Rida was a free-spirited child, friendly with everybody. She has always thought the sexual assault took away her trust in humanity. She is very clear that she considers herself a strong survivor, not a victim. "Yes, it has affected me in seminal ways, but this alone does not define me. I have fought and continue to fight it, but I have not let it consume me in a manner that keeps me closed to absorbing other experiences. Life is not over because of it and never will be."

Her sister, who went through exactly the same ordeal, is comfortable in her own skin, happily married, and insists that the trauma doesn't affect her. I believe both. I also believe we can't really know. It's impossible to tease out all the variables—our innate personalities, the things that happen to us, and the people we become are all so bound up with each other.

Remember Souhayla in Iraq, whose despair is so debilitating that she cannot even open her eyes. Imagine being an old person in a nursing home, or trapped in a relative's house, with rape the final drama of your life. Imagine being in a strange country with a rapist who has married you and locked up your passport. Imagine being a child with a secret for which there are no words, only dark shapes sliding around in your vision, shapes nobody else sees.

Imagine what would be unleashed if so many people didn't have to waste so much time dealing with flashbacks, secret-keeping, suicidal thoughts, low self-esteem, crippling fear of ... everything, and on down the dreary list. Imagine the fantastic, the amazing, the mind-boggling things so many rape survivors could do, say, create or be if they didn't have to waste time being traumatized and stymied and made small. Imagine the art that we could create, the songs we could sing, the forests we could plant, the life-changing planet-saving gizmos we could invent, instead of wasting our time trying to stop our hearts from pounding if we hear footsteps behind us on our way to the bus stop. It's such a wholesale waste of potential.

So next time you hear or read anything about how men who rape shouldn't have their lives fall apart because of "a few minutes," stop in your tracks, howl with outrage, and then go do something joyful.

21

Lead weights for drowning

Am I unlovable? Am I ridiculous? Do people look at me and not respect me?

—Audrey

LIFE, UNLIKE GOLF, doesn't allow for handicaps when you go out to play. You come yowling out into the world into a random set of circumstances, and they mark you forever, for better or worse.

"I grew up in a very abusive household although I had no idea that that was the case," Heather told me. Her mother was "a narcissistic person. My personality wasn't my own. I was her puppet. My entire life was me trying to fit the perfect mold, but there was no perfect mold. Dad was verbally and physically abusive. But it didn't seem weird to me."

Nor did her abusive relationship with the boy she'd been friends with since middle school. It was only when she was twenty, after she had escaped to college in another city (having applied in secret, knowing she wouldn't be allowed to leave if she asked) that "seeing how 'normal' people lived, it hit me like a ton of bricks that this was not the norm.

"I decided to end the relationship I was in. I met up with him and broke up with him. He was not happy I ended it. When I got home, my parents had already found out. They were so pissed at me that they kicked me out of the house. I grabbed my suitcase, threw it in my car, drove to a local mall parking lot, and spent the night in the car.

"Late night/early morning, there was a knock on the passenger window. I looked up and saw that it was my ex. I cracked the door. The next thing I know I'm being dragged out of the car and slammed onto the ground.

"There were nine guys. Four I had known. The other five were strangers. One was my best friend's boyfriend. Some had bats. One had a gun. They kicked me and beat me. They zip-tied me and put me in the trunk. They took me to a basement and took turns raping me.

"One of the guys dropped me back off at my car. I didn't really know what to do. I wanted to call my best friend, but one of them was her boyfriend. I hesitated to do that. I threw better clothes on, waited for the mall to open, cleaned myself up in the bathroom. I had broken ribs, cuts and bruises. I drove to a friend's house, the mother of someone I had nannied for. I asked to use the shower. I said it was my dad who hurt me."

It was nine years ago that Heather was raped. Since then, she has had to repeat a year of college (she failed because she just couldn't concentrate), change her career (her original plan was too rooted in painful memories), spend thousands of dollars on therapy, negotiate new relationships with everyone in her life, and find a new center. All this without any support from her family.

Rape is terrible no matter what, but the more stories I hear, the more I see the huge power of family, support, childhood messages. I have plenty of baggage myself, but I'm convinced that the reason it was possible for me to become a person who is happy to be in the world is because I had the safety net so many victims lack.

Heather's father threw her out when she didn't do things his way. And, before that, abuse was her "normal," so she didn't even know how to distinguish a respectful relationship from a degrading one.

I think of my father throwing out, not his daughter, but about a dozen policemen who didn't believe me. I think of my mother printing copies of my *New York Times* op-ed and handing them out to shocked visitors. I think of my brother, my friend and my boyfriend starting a group called Men Against Sexual Assault in the 1980s and sallying forth to talk to astonished high school boys. I think of my cousins in Bombay who played music for me constantly for days after the rape, doing their best to drown out the hateful voices in my head. I think of so many friends who never, ever made me feel bad or weird or ashamed. I just want to get them all together in an unabashed love fest, and fling orchids and chocolates at them.

Latisha, like Heather, grew up in a verbally abusive household. Her mother was drunk all the time, and Latisha hated going home. Hers was in a rough urban neighborhood. She was raped twice. The first time, a cute fellow high school student, slapped her in the face and told her to shut the fuck up, raped her, and took away the borrowed gold chain she was wearing. She told me that she was more upset about the chain than the rape, which she managed to block out of her mind for a long time. The rapist talked about her in the locker room and showed the chain to his buddies. It took her twenty-five years to acknowledge to herself that he had raped her. During that time, he was murdered in prison, where he was doing time for some other crime.

Later, she was raped again while she was keeping out of the house to avoid her mother's boyfriend. "My mom drank," she told me. "I was the second mother, taking care of my brothers. I had been in caretaker mode since I was a young kid. Because of the verbal abuse, I never had any self-worth. I was constantly torn down."

Nobody is immune from rape. But everybody has different tools in his/her/their bag to either cope with it, or to make coping that bit harder. Stones in your pocket make it easier to drown.

22

A brief pause for *ennui*

I JUST READ a delightful book called *Mozart's Starling*, by Lyanda Lynn Haupt.[88] She writes about Mozart's pet starling, how it fitted into his life and music, and about Carmen, her own adopted starling. The book explores serious issues of language, communication, inspiration and environment, but it is such a fun read from beginning to end.

I am overcome with envy. *That's* the book I want to be writing today. I want to write about Vienna, and birdsong, and Mozart's Piano Concerto Number 17 in G major, and starlings sitting on my head... Art! Joy! Life! It's so much more inviting than discussing getting gonorrhoea from one's older brother, or rape as a weapon of war.

And yet, here we are, in a world that includes both birdsong and brutality.

23

The quality of mercy

*"You'll die, you'll die," I screamed inside. "You will
rot and stink and cave in on yourself. God will give
you to me. Your bones will melt and your blood will
catch fire. I'll rip you open and feed you to the dogs.
Like in the Bible, like the way it ought to be, God will
give you to me. God will give you to me!"*

—Dorothy Allison, *Bastard Out of Carolina*

VENGEANCE IS such a delicious thought. When one woman
told her daughter about her long-ago rape, the daughter
was so furious that she wanted to find the man and kill him.
My mother, historically non-violent, spoke longingly about
dipping the men who raped me in boiling oil. One woman
wrote to me after my 2013 op-ed: "Gosh, they should be
stoned to death for doing this to you."

When I read Dorothy Allison's writing decades ago, it thrilled me. It still does. Anger is underrated, when it comes to feeling alive and worthy again. But so is forgiveness, which gets a bad rap from people like me who tend to sneer at namby-pamby religious concepts and think they are for weaklings.

As I look around at this wicked world, though, more and more I see that the real heroes include those who can forgive—others and themselves. That is why I was riveted by the story of Thordis Elva and Tom Stranger.

Thordis was a sixteen-year-old high-schooler in Iceland. Tom was an exchange student from Australia. They had a teen romance, which abruptly ended when he raped her one night. Years later, after much trauma and suffering, Thordis emailed Tom, not at all confident that he would reply. He did, and admitted what he had done and how much he had been haunted by it.

The two met in the middle—literally. They both flew to South Africa and spent some time coming to terms with the rape. They co-wrote a book, *South of Forgiveness*,[89] and gave a TED talk in February 2017.[90]

Their presentation is fascinating. Imagine! Imagine your rapist admitting that what he did was rape, and taking responsibility for it. I can't imagine. And I, you, and the textbooks can all insist until we turn blue that it shouldn't matter what the rapist thinks, but hearing from Tom is amazing.

At TED, Thordis said, "I was raised in a world where girls are taught that they get raped for a reason ... I disavowed the truth by convincing myself it was sex, not rape."

Tom said, "I sank the memories deep and I tied a rock to them ... I gripped tight to the simple notion that I wasn't a bad person... I didn't think this was in my bones. I thought I was made of something else."

From their book:

Tom described how he felt deserving of my body that night, without any concern for me, and consequently convinced himself that what he did was sex and not rape. The following nine years were marked by denial, in which he did his best to outrun the past, until I confronted him in a pivotal email that changed our lives for ever.

By the time Thordis came to terms with what had happened, Tom had returned to the other end of the globe, out of range of the Icelandic justice system. In any case, seventy percent of rape cases in Iceland were dismissed, even when there was physical proof, which Thordis did not have.

Thordis and Tom maintain that the essence of their story is not forgiveness, but responsibility. They focus on the perpetrator's responsibility, and the importance of turning our gaze in that direction rather than at the victim.

I want to be very careful here, as they no doubt were when they wrote and rewrote their book. When I say it's amazing, I do not mean that Tom is amazing. It's amazing that he 'fessed up, but he did what he needed to do to live with himself. He will still forever be a man who committed rape, who deliberately hurt someone he cared about. However, I do respect people who evolve, who can face themselves, and for that I tip my hat to him.

But mostly I tip my hat to her. And when I watched the video, I had a surprising emotion: envy. Envy that she had the courage to face exactly what happened, and the good fortune to be able to work it out *with the person who caused it*.

What terrible vengeance would I want to wreak if I could have those four men in the room with me? I think I would want what Thordis got: to talk. It would probably be a spectacular failure. I don't think they will have evolved and I would not expect them to think they had done anything wrong. They were very sure that I got what was coming to me.

But I would like to hear from them. I want to know so many things. Perhaps I shouldn't care, but I do. Did they mean it when they said they would kill me if I told anyone, or did I just live in fear for years for nothing? Did they keep track of me? Were they pleased with themselves? Did they even think about that day after it was over?

And when it was my turn, how satisfying it would be to wave my writing in their faces, to tell them how wrong they were, to explain that I thrived and that I did not for a moment learn the lesson they tried so roughly to teach me.

There's no "right" way to heal. I say, if someone violated you and you want to follow Dorothy Allison's lead, rip him open and feed him to the dogs—I won't stand in your way. If you want to beat him to a pulp, plaster his picture all over a local telephone pole or internet forum, poison his garden, shit on his front porch, put a really creative curse on him, destroy his reputation, ruin his life … go for it, sister. Forgiveness just seems like a powerful option to consider.

"Forgiveness is the only way, I tell myself, because, whether or not he deserves my forgiveness, I deserve peace," Thordis declared during the TED talk.

Thordis and Tom's collaboration was greeted with anger and contempt by some people. When they spoke together at the Royal Festival Hall in London, shouting protesters gathered outside the building with placards. "There's a rapist in the building! Get the rapist out!" they cried. One man tweeted: "It's disrespectful to survivors and we don't live in a culture where rapists need to be humanized."

I disagree. I think we have to start by humanizing rapists, not to downplay their actions but to face the fact that rapists *are* human. That makes the crime worse, not better. Humans have choices, and rape is a horrible one.

I don't understand the protests. Here is a rapist who says, "I raped." This is noteworthy. When even women who are raped have a hard time calling it what it is, what are the chances of a man who committed date rape owning up to what he did?

I'm not in the least bit sorry for Tom Stranger. I'm glad people yelled at him. He chose to admit his crime, but doing so doesn't mitigate the pain he caused. I also hope lots of other men heard the protesters. I am completely sure he wasn't the only rapist in the building that day, and it gives me great pleasure to think about men walking by, or working in the building, or in the audience, feeling a tad uncomfortable as they perhaps recalled a time they had committed sexual assault but never admitted it to anyone.

There's something both frightening and exhilarating about a man, an ordinary man, saying, "I raped." It's frightening because it gives the lie to the "Monster" theory of rape, that keeps perpetrators in the "other" category. I can't even distance the men who raped me, who seemed monstrous and behaved that way, who were from a different class, who pretty much checked all the boxes of stoned savages on a mountaintop wreaking mayhem, probably had families they went home to, parents they obeyed or didn't, dreams they had or hadn't, little vanities and delusions. They were just boys. Being boys. That's frightening.

But it's also exhilarating because if the Monster is Us, then the Monster is capable of learning and growth. Even if the vast majority of men who rape are either proud or in denial, here is one who sees what he did and is sorry. That is something, a small sliver of possibility.

I've noticed a funny disconnect in people's reactions to rape. Globally, two completely different attitudes often exist simultaneously. One says it's just rape and not really on a par with "serious" crimes. The other is immediately violent. Hang them, burn them, castrate them. I can't speak for other women, but, for me, the angry reactions of men in my life were difficult and intimidating. When one man said he would like to beat them to a pulp, I felt sick. After what I'd just been through, I didn't want to think about any violence towards anyone, ever again. His words made me feel as threatened and weirdly commodified as the rapists had. Once again, men wanted to work something out through me. I wanted no part of it. My father, who never said a word about vengeance, but instead woke me up every morning after the rape by stroking my face, did so much more to make me feel safe.

More than 250 young girls accused sports doctor Larry Nassar of sexually assaulting them.[91] They trusted him, and were rewarded with betrayal on a spectacular scale. It was deeply gratifying to watch the live stream of woman after woman facing him in court and saying what was in her heart: "You took advantage of my innocence and trust. You were my doctor. Why?" Nassar responded by writing a letter to the judge where he declared, "Hell hath no fury like a woman scorned." There's no question that he's a despicable creep who deserves to spend the rest of his life in misery. But I *still* can't relate to the people who have said on record that he deserves to be raped in prison. If rape is always undeserved, then even Larry Nassar doesn't deserve it.

During the TED talk, discussing how it is important to understand that victims are people and so are rapists, Thordis said, "How will we understand what it is in human societies that produces violence if we refuse to recognize the humanity of those who commit it? And can we empower survivors if we're making them feel 'less than'? How can we discuss solutions to one of the biggest threats to the lives of women and children around the world, if the very words we use are part of the problem?"

24

Your rape is worse than mine

Nothing is more isolating than having a particular history. At least that's what I thought. Now I know: All pain is the same. Only the details are different.

—Kevin Powers, *The Yellow Birds*

I AM SITTING in a Mumbai suburb with Kalki Koechlin, and she is telling me about the sexual abuse she lived through as a child. I am aghast at what I'm hearing.

I thank her for telling me her story, and say I cannot imagine how she has come so far in working through it. I cannot conceive how awful it must have been.

"I can't imagine going through *your* experience!" she says. "I can't think of anything worse."

There's something slightly unhinged about the scene: two grown women each insisting that the other deserves the prize for Worst Rape.

Is one rape worse than the other? This is a ridiculous question. Why do we insist on ranking sexual assault? Survivors do it to our own discredit. I remember sitting in a support group and thinking to myself that "my" rape wasn't as bad as those of the other poor losers.

No matter how many stories, no matter how many victims, I'm always appalled afresh. It always sounds so terrible. "Mine" always seems more manageable.

I'm not sure why we do this. It's a weird phenomenon that I have seen over and over. In my experience, only individuals do it. Put us in a group, and we humans are usually eager to claim the mantle of victimhood. "Collective victimhood"[92] is well documented. But, when it comes to sitting in a room on an August afternoon and talking about rape with a fellow survivor, I'm always aghast and appalled, and convinced that the other person suffered more than me.

Perhaps there's some defense mechanism at work. If someone else is worse off, suddenly what you're dealing with isn't so bad. It doesn't always work, of course—after I had two miscarriages and one man helpfully told me about his wife's six failed pregnancies, I just wanted to put my head in a pressure cooker and boil it. But sometimes it does.

I'm not wholly convinced about my defense mechanism theory. I know how bad my rape was, but everyone else's still seems worse. I don't think it's because I'm trying to downplay my story. It's because I *know* my story. I know it beyond the few sentences I've written, or the words I've used to describe it to so many people over the years. I know the tiny little details (although by now it's pretty hazy—a rather wonderful side effect of time). I know what they did and I know what I felt and I know how bad it was. But I know I made it through. When you experience something first-hand, you know its colors and smells and the full horror of the hands pulling off your shoes. But you also know the limits of your pain and suffering. You don't have to wonder. And reality, no matter how bad, is more manageable than unknown horror. I was never in Kalki's position, so how do I know I would have survived? I *know* I survived what happened to me. No matter how bad it was, here I am. Here is the East River flowing outside my window. Here is a bowl of pomegranate seeds deeply, joyously red. Here is a little plastic pig that my spouse gave me when we first met. Here is my brother wearing a suit and tie, looking seriously at me in a photo that always cracks me up for some reason. Here I am. No matter what happened, here I am.

Whatever the reason, ranking rapes is a prime example of the magical thinking that swirls around rape. Seems like no matter how rational we are, when it comes to life's big things—death, pain, birth, love—we quickly revert to charms and chants and magic potions. So what if it doesn't work?

For a short time before I learned the actual statistics on rape, I thought I was safe because, now that it had happened to me, my turn was over. I was out of the running—been there, done that. This was a great comfort, until it hit me that of course you are right back in the running—rapists don't go around asking victims whether they've already had their turn.

Michelle Hattingh wrote her thesis on rape in her home country, South Africa. On the morning she defended it, she spoke about how a South African woman has a higher chance of being raped than of learning to read. She did well. That evening, she went out to celebrate her success—and was raped on the beach near the party.

Hattingh wrote a book[93] about her experience. I wonder if, while she was working on her thesis, she did a little magical thinking of her own, and thought that writing about rape made her immune. I can't know what she was thinking, but I, too, wrote about rape for both my undergraduate and graduate theses. I know that a part of me believed, and still believes, that if I just own it and know it and figure it out, then it can't happen to me again.

And if it happened to me, then it can't happen to my child. Now there's an extreme example of magical thinking. We all know that we ultimately can't protect our children, but we never stop pretending we can. It's too difficult not to. Having a child really brings home the reality that there is indeed something much worse than whatever happened to you—someone hurting this small, magnificent person who depends on you.

While it serves no useful purpose to rank pain and suffering, we do. And of course rapes do fall into some categories—being held by warlords and gang-raped for years just isn't in the same box as being raped by a stranger where you live, and going straight to the hospital. That's true. But you can't predict which woman will be able to come to terms with it sooner. Will the marital rape survivor build a new life faster than the incest survivor? Will the young Kenyan flower-farmer raped by the farm manager find peace sooner than the sixty-five-year-old white woman whose assailant broke into her apartment and raped her?

It's very delicate, this balancing act: to acknowledge that rape is just ghastly, and to simultaneously assert that it is simply one of many ghastly things. Indian lawyer and activist Flavia Agnes, writing about marital rape (and I'm not going to waste any space here wondering if marital rape exists; let's get real) addresses this:

I don't believe in placing rape on a pedestal within the hierarchy of crimes within a marriage. For a woman who is facing domestic violence, it is equally violating if her skull is fractured, her spine is broken, her cornea is damaged, her liver is injured, or her vagina is penetrated forcefully. What women object to is the violence involved. [94]

Perhaps we have a basic need to rank things. Kevin O'Donnell, sexually abused for years by his mother's boyfriend Frank, speaks to different groups about his experience. He talks about the death of his infant daughter: "I thought watching our first child die, carrying her nine-month-old body out to a waiting hearse and placing her in a body bag was the worst thing I could ever have experienced in my life … I was wrong again. There was something worse and I didn't even realize it at the time … Keeping that little secret about Frank was worse."

I had a moment of shock reading this. After a lifetime of telling anyone who'd listen that rape isn't the worst possible thing to happen, of fighting a culture that calls rape victims "living corpses," it would never have occurred to me that it was worse than the death of a child. But for Kevin, it was. That is his truth—*his* truth, not the one society foisted on him.

Kevin elaborated for me. "When Jenna Rose died I knew it was inevitable, and once it happened I had family and friends to share the grief and sadness. With the abuse it was like being locked up in a cell for twenty-five years with no one to talk to and work out the grief, sadness and isolation."

For me, the death of my father was worse than being raped, although fathers are supposed to die and children are not. But, unlike Kevin, I wasn't abused for years by someone who should have been looking out for me. Maybe the childhood rape was worse because it was a malign act, whereas the child's death was not in human control. Maybe... See, here I go, comparing again. Why do we waste time thinking about what should be worse? It's a futile mind-game.

I do have one absolute: the worst rape is the one you don't survive. Jyoti Singh fought her attackers, and that rightfully makes her a hero. I would never say, or think, that she should have lain there and taken it. She might have died either way. My point is that there is no wrong way to react, but there is a worst-case outcome: you don't get a chance to carry on.

In Alice Sebold's powerful novel *The Lovely Bones*, the protagonist Susie Salmon is raped and murdered, and the book is told from her point of view. Reviewers loved it; so did I. But there was a fatal flaw—the wonderful heroine is *dead*. I don't care how feisty and insightful and wise and unforgettable you are—once you're dead, you've lost.

Marital rape. Incest. The drunk boyfriend, the family friend. For me, being gang-raped on a mountain by drug-addled would-be killers seems far preferable to any of these. Crazy, but true. I could leave the mountain behind, tell myself it had nothing to do with my safe world. But anyone I know who has been raped by someone he or she knows is as aghast at my story as I was at Kalki's. Magical thinking. I know it makes no sense, but I still think your rape is worse than mine.

25

Good girls don't

"Confound it!" cried the Doctor, "my wife has for-gotten to have the buttons on my white waistcoat changed. Ah, women!"

—Marcel Proust, *Cities of the Plain*, 1921, Part 2, Ch. 2

FOR A BRIEF and nasty moment, I was a high-school student in Massachusetts. I was mentally far away most of the time, but a few things did make an impression: a cute boy named Bobby, the room full of books that my English teacher allowed me to ransack, and an assembly during which we watched a short film on how not to be raped. The part I recall involved a manly voiceover telling us to run if we felt threatened, but, if we couldn't run, then the best way to deter a rapist was to either defecate or throw up. That would turn the Bad Guys off, by offending their delicate sensibilities.

Months later, when I was being held down and trying to get out alive and unharmed, I remembered this advice—the only advice I'd ever received from anyone about rape. I don't know about you who are reading this, but I'm definitely not one whose bowels loosen when threatened. I'm a proud member of Team Constipation Under Stress. As for throwing up, same thing—I shut down rather than spew. So I felt like a failure when I couldn't do the two things I had been instructed to do.

In retrospect, it was probably a good thing. The rapists might have been put off, true, or they might have been further enraged and ended up killing us after all. But it was another reason for me to feel I could have somehow performed better, somehow stopped it, when the truth is that the only people who are truly responsible for preventing rape are rapists.

Who gets raped? Who do we *think* gets raped? Are girls who can shit and vomit on command immune? What about sex workers? Even if we acknowledge that anyone can be raped, who *deserves* to be raped? When are we willing to call it rape? At what point do you lose the sympathy of your peers? When you've drunk too much, when you've had sex with x number of men in the past, when you're just not a nice person?

Rida, who was molested by a grown man when she was a toddler, said, "I always dressed in shorts. Was it my fault?"

"The defense lawyer said there was interest on both sides," Audrey told me, explaining why the case against the men who raped her was dismissed. "He used the fact that I had had sex before."

#MeToo took off in a big way after I started writing this book, and it makes me wildly happy to be able to say that the conversation about who gets raped is clearly shifting, at least in some parts of some societies. I hope it makes its way to more bedrooms, boardrooms and courtrooms very soon. In the media, for all the daily barrage of sexism and misogyny, I've seen increasingly nuanced portrayals of rape survivors. *Broadchurch*, a British TV crime series, spent an entire season dealing with a rape case. The victim was intoxicated when she was raped, and the police officers on the show treated her with sensitivity.

Talking about this stuff gets tricky. Talking about "prevention" is tricky, because, if we know that the fault lies with the men who rape, why should we talk with women and girls about prevention at all? If we tell our daughters (and sons) how to keep themselves safe, aren't we also saying that it's their own fault if something happens?

Audrey struggled with this for a long time. "Women are human," she says now. "We are not perfect, and we can make poor decisions. But the only ones responsible for sexual assault are those who choose to rape."

One of my colleagues at the Boston Area Rape Crisis Center taught a self-defense class for women, and for a long time I resisted signing up. I felt that if I signed up to learn to defend myself, then I was saying that somehow I was responsible for not defending myself the first time. I was saying that I was a hapless fool lying there on the mountain just letting myself be raped. I should have twirled madly around with my cape flying in the wind, kicked them in the balls, dropped them, thrust my sword into their throats, flung them off the mountain, spat on my blade to clean it, and marched triumphantly home, not a hair out of place.

Eventually I took the class, telling myself that learning to protect myself in certain situations didn't mean it was my responsibility to not be raped. But it is tricky—how do I talk to my daughter about being as safe as she can be, and at the same time raise a feminist who knows exactly where the buck stops?

We want to teach our daughters to write their own destinies, but what happens when they insist on taking the responsibility for bad things that happen to them? The adolescent daughter of family friends became embroiled with a paedophile who persuaded her to pose naked for him, and then sold her photos online. He is in prison now, and she is angry at her parents because she insists that *she* seduced *him*, and he doesn't deserve to be incarcerated. When she first connected with him, she was twelve.

In September 2017, *Vice* ran a photo essay[95] about older women taking self-defense classes in Korogocho and Kibera, two Nairobi slums. Rape is widespread in their community, and older women are particular targets. The photographs are inspiring—women in their fifties, sixties and seventies practising their kicks and punches, looking powerful in their wrinkles and bright prints. I think it's great, and love the fantasy of some young hoodlum being kicked into the gutter by a ferocious granny. But there's always the part of me that says, why should they have to, and what good is a swift kick when you're faced with an armed gang? Why not give boys courses in not raping instead?

Why not both? There is a course for boys, in fact—it's called Your Moment of Truth, and the NGO Ujamaa Africa offers it in those very same slums. Boys learn about consent and how to stand up against violence against women.

Ultimately, I say yes to anything that increases your confidence and makes you feel strong. If my kid wanted to take a self-defense class to lessen her chances of being attacked, I'd sign her up, but throw in a long, convoluted, confusing lecture about how she should trust her instinct in dangerous situations, not be sidetracked by the voice in her head telling her to shit or vomit or kick. And then I'd throw in another lecture about how self-defense courses are all fine, but she is not responsible for preventing rape—men are. And then...I would get an eye-roll and *"Amma, stop!"*

As parents, most of us want to teach our children respect—for themselves, for other people. We want to teach them how to stand up for themselves, for other people, for the right thing. We can't do this alone, so we look to the community, the academy, the institutions that regulate our world for help. And sometimes we find it in the oddest places.

Growing up in Bombay, I went to convent school, which was quite ordinary for a Muslim girl whose parents wanted her to get a good education. The nuns ran a tight ship. They devoted themselves to increasing our knowledge and the length of our uniform skirts. They also paid great attention to our morals and reputations. I loved the nuns. They taught us about integrity and discipline and those lessons have stayed with me. However, despite helping raise strong girls, their gender politics were very suspect.

We were required to attend "moral science" classes, where we learned how to behave. We learned about the horror of Boys. Boys were to be avoided at all costs, especially after we became women, as explained in a little booklet about menstruation. I can't remember anything about the booklet except its enticing cover, which was glossy and colorful. (In those days everything in India was published on cheap newsprint, and this little booklet from abroad with a gleaming picture of a white girl in pigtails was hypnotic. I saved it for years. I think I might have been slightly in love with the girl in pigtails.) The nun teaching moral science told us in no uncertain terms that socializing with Boys would be our downfall. We must avoid Boys under any circumstances. In fact, if they ever saw us outside school in the company of a Boy, any Boy, we would be expelled, no questions asked.

The message was loud and clear: if anything untoward ever happened to one of us at the hands of a Boy, it would be our fault. End of lesson.

Kasia Urbaniak is not a nun. Her platform leather boots are unlike anything the nuns in Loreto Convent ever wore (at least in our presence). I read about her in the news. She worked as a dominatrix for seventeen years, and now she runs workshops for women. She teaches them how to assert themselves in uncomfortable situations with men, from the guy who assumes you'll make his coffee to the one who corners you behind his desk after everyone else has gone home. She honed her techniques during her years of working in a dungeon, when she had to learn to overcome "the moment of speechlessness, of neuromuscular lockdown"[96] that we all know so well when we are suddenly put on the spot.

I think about my beloved nuns at Loreto Convent, and then about a former whip-wielding sex worker in New York City. If I had to send my daughter or nephews to one or the other to learn about sexual equality and righteous behavior, I would choose the dominatrix.

Wow. I just wrote that. I hope I don't go to hell. Forgive me, Mother Ursula.

Yes, it's fraught. Who do we think gets raped?

In her manuscript, Yasmin El-Rifae describes a scene where a victim of mob sexual assault endured a virginity test sanctioned by police and lawyers:

"I don't understand," Sarah says. "What use is it to them, to do a virginity exam like that?"

"I guess it works for them either way," T. says. "If they find a hymen, then they can see that nothing happened under their watch."

"And if they don't, then it's still all good, because non-virgins can't be raped anyway, right," Sarah says.

Ay, as Hamlet would say, there's the rub! We still persist in thinking some women can't be raped. Especially "bad" women. If bad women are raped, it doesn't fit our victim narrative, and so we'd rather ignore it. Or call it sex.

I met some sex workers in rural Sangli, Maharashtra, hub of turmeric, sugarcane, and formerly of HIV. Almost every one—male, female, trans, gender-fluid, gay, straight, bi—had multiple stories of rape. Gang-raped by eleven of his lover's friends on a hotel terrace; set upon by more than a dozen of her brother's political rivals in a forest; raped by policemen as the price of staying out of prison and earning money for her children… "The police say, you can't be raped because you have sex all day," one woman told me. As for the men, every single thing is stacked against them. Gay sex is illegal in India in any case, plus Indian law only recognizes the rape of cis women: females who were assigned female at birth.

Meena Seshu of SANGRAM is one of the co-authors of "The Right(s) Evidence,"[97] a 2015 survey of sex workers (women, men and transgender) in Asia that explored, among other things, sexual violence in their lives. I interviewed her for my column in *Mint*, expecting to highlight some of the report's fascinating findings. Instead, the bigger story turned out to be the global reaction, or rather non-reaction, "absolute and total silence":

"It was launched in Bangkok—nobody wrote about it. It was launched in Myanmar—nobody wrote about it. The UN distributes it—nobody writes about it. The media came to all the events. People from TV, people from newspapers—they interviewed people like the study's interviewers, who were all sex workers themselves. And then nobody wrote about it." [...] At the Myanmar launch, there was an excellent press note, sex workers and other experts were available for stories, and nobody wrote a thing. "What are they so scared about?" wonders Seshu.[98]

Kiran wore a rather fabulous sparkly green blouse on the day we spent together. She took me to Gokulnagar, where she and other sex workers live and work in colorful houses set in a row backing on to an undeveloped parcel of land. It was a peaceful morning scene, with kids running around, smells of cooking and washing, women clustered around a sleeping newborn baby. The baby was so cute I pulled out my camera to take a picture, only to be smacked down. It's bad luck to take pictures of babies with their eyes closed.

Kiran is from a high-caste Hindu family in a village far away from here. Her birth family is political, connected, and influential. Her brother was the local *sarpanch*, head of the *panchayat*, the village government. He was embroiled in a political dispute, and his rivals caught Kiran, fifteen at the time, put her in a car, took her into the jungle, and raped her.

They raped her, kicked her, urinated on her: "It was very bad, very bad." She still has scars on her back where thorns pierced her flesh. They left her there and roared off. She picked herself up and knew that if she went back home she would either be murdered or driven to suicide by her family.

Certainly nobody would ever want to marry her. She never went home. She walked in the other direction. Now she does sex work for a living. Her children are grown and doing well. She has several lovers and is content with her life. She takes no nonsense from anyone.

The sex workers in her town get very indignant at those who would either pity them or "save" them. When I was in Gokulnagar, a government car drove up with two men in it. One was a police officer and one a court official. They were looking for information about a sex worker they had detained a few weeks ago, alerted by a tip from the Freedom Firm, an anti-slavery group that, supported by religious Americans, likes to "rescue" women, lock them up, take away their children, and generally turn a blind eye to any nuances that distinguish between actual trafficking and sex work out of choice.

Trafficking involves lies, coercion, the buying and selling of others—for sex or a variety of other things. Sex work is choosing to sell sex for money as the best option available to you.

Melissa Ditmore [99] has researched human trafficking in many countries, and is an expert in this distinction. "Human trafficking," she told me, "inherently involves force, fraud, or coercion in any labor sector, and has been documented in fisheries, agriculture, domestic work, and many other labor sectors. Trafficking victims include people of all ages and genders. Sex work is foremost an income-generating activity, in which money is paid for sexual services such as prostitution, stripping, and pornography. Sex workers negotiate what they will do, what it will cost, and decline to work with people they do not want to interact with. Trafficked persons in the sex trades typically do not have these options, but many people trafficked into prostitution return to sex work when they have escaped trafficking situations, because sex work may earn more than other options open to them.

"When sex work is conflated with trafficking, few victims are helped because jobs in which trafficking is common are neglected when anti-trafficking efforts focus on the sex trades. Sex workers suffer the brunt of police raids, but trafficked women in the sex trades have told me about being arrested as many as ten times without being recognized as trafficking victims by law enforcement.

"Minors are not believed to be able to consent to participation in the sex trades … all instances of prostitution by someone under eighteen years of age are defined as trafficking."

"Anti-slavery" organizations set out to rescue trafficked and sexually exploited minors, but, lacking nuance and basic respect, they often "rescue" adult sex workers, separate them from their children, and put them in situations of greater vulnerability by cutting off their livelihoods and bringing them under the jurisdiction of the police.[100] Their missionary zeal consists of a thin veneer of righteousness covering a seething disdain for women. Their "rescues" too often leave out the real victims of trafficking. Equating all sex work with rape does nobody any favors.

Sangeeta asked, "Who makes the laws? Did anybody ask us? They call us *bechaare* (pathetic). Why don't they look after the ones who really are *bechaare*?"

Sangeeta is a second-generation sex worker. She would have liked to do something else, but she couldn't finish school because of the abuse she got for being a sex worker's daughter. Her teacher threatened to burn her alive, and she left school and became a sex worker at twelve. She lives with her children and sister. She talked about feeling safe working out of her upstairs room, rather than visiting clients. "If a client calls me somewhere else, and suddenly four or five men appear, that's rape. *Jaan bhi to bachaani hai.* I have to save my life." This has happened to her. Now that she's part of SANGRAM's sisterhood, however, she and her fellow sex workers look out for each other. They even got together and stopped a man who used to constantly harass them. "He used to curse, spit, kick the women in passing. We tied him up, put chilli powder in his eyes, and beat him soundly. No more harassment."

These women aren't "good" by society's standards, but they are powerful. Maybe that's part of what makes them scary.

Indian wives are supposed to enter marriage as innocent virgins. They exist for men's pleasure, not their own. I heard the story of one woman who got carried away while having sex with her husband. In her excitement and passion, she got on top of him. He left her the next day, saying that her enjoyment of sex showed she was experienced and "spoiled."

Maybe acknowledging that all sorts of women get raped by all sorts of men messes too much with the comfortable narrative, the narrative that says only good girls get raped. Oh, but it also says good girls *don't* get raped. Both these things can't be true, and sex workers aren't good girls, so how can they be raped, and if they're raped, they're human and hurt, and we can't have that, so let's just shut our eyes and maybe the whole confusing thing will go away.

What makes a "good" girl? Too often, being good means being docile, passive, accepting your lot without question.

I hope, in that case, for a new generation of only bad girls, who listen to themselves and follow their own hearts. And get up and straddle their lovers with abandon.

The rural sex workers I met are not typical. They are organized. Sex workers the world over put up with tremendous abuse, oppression and exploitation. These women and men have also endured oppression that could easily crush any human being. Child marriage, constant beatings, violence and put-downs, and nobody, including yourself, with any faith that you might be a human being of worth and value. They have survived all this, and somehow, by coming together, they have come to believe in their own worth and value. They have even managed something that is all too rare among much more privileged women: having some power and agency around sex.

Meena put it well: "We have notions of patriarchy that are set in gold and stone. The sex workers have kicked the ass of these notions."

When you can take or leave lovers at will, when you can say no to sex because the man who is paying you refuses to put on a condom, when you know that if someone gets too rough you can beat on the wall and half a dozen women will come to your aid, when you can demand pleasure for yourself, you have more sexual agency than many a married woman living in luxury. It's counter-intuitive but true: women at the very bottom of society, the truly reviled and crushed, have somehow managed to carve out a breathing space for themselves that includes sexual liberation, despite their continuing vulnerability to rape. They are not the ones who have to pay the going rate to sex workers to get sexual satisfaction. They don't have to hide their lusts and fantasies. They don't have to be "good".

But they—like convent girls, like women who go out to nightclubs, like grandmothers in Nairobi, like trans people staying out of the glare of streetlights—are trapped by the same narrative, the narrative that refuses to acknowledge that, no matter who you are, if someone forces you to have sex, *it is rape*. The narrative that says: good girls don't get raped; bad girls can't get raped. In either case, the nuns' infamous Boys are off the hook. We've created a narrative that says that either it didn't happen to you, or you deserved it.

26

Rape prevention for beginners

FOR THOSE who would feel better prepared if there were a rape prevention formula to follow, I offer my own:

- Stay home; avoid strangers.
- Go out; avoid family.
- Look fierce.
- Look meek.
- Be loud.
- Be soft.
- Smile.
- Don't smile.
- Be friendly.
- Be unfriendly.
- Be bold.
- Be cold.
- Be young.
- Be old.

- Lock up your vagina.
- Lock up your children.
- Lock up your thoughts.
- Defuse.
- Disappear.
- Die.

27

Boys will...

The judge etc. said they were normal men, how could they be criminals? But if normal men mugged someone, they would be criminals.

—Audrey

Men, if you say you're a feminist, then fuck like a feminist.

—Samantha Bee

WHO RAPES? Just as we can have fixed ideas about victims, we have them about perpetrators as well.

Are all men capable of rape? In my own life, I cannot accept this. Here is what one man said when I asked him if he thought he could imagine raping someone. "For myself, I would say no," he said. "There's a level of empathy that would make it impossible for me." I believed him.

I can imagine murdering, but not raping. Murder is worse than rape, I know, but there are lots of reasons to do it. If I were in a state of out-of-control rage, if someone were threatening to harm me or someone else, if killing someone were the only way to avoid some terrible catastrophe... I know, this is a weird, weird paragraph. But think about it—there is *no reasonable reason* to rape. You're either doing it explicitly to cause damage, or because you want sex and don't understand or care that the other person does not want it.

Justifiable homicide exists (for instance, if you're killing someone to stop a rape), but justifiable rape? Do you ever need to rape someone to stop any other crime? The only people who openly justify rape are those who run blatantly woman-hating societies, where women are objects.

Speaking of which, let's talk about objectification. In my days of clarity and righteousness as a college student, I wholeheartedly believed the conventional feminist wisdom that men objectify women in order to rape them. The logic goes like this: if you deny someone's humanity, you can abuse them.

But perhaps it's your *own* humanity you have to deny. Or at least your own positive humanity. Cruelty and sadism are also very human.

Social scientists Alan Fiske and Tage Rai have studied the moral motivations of violence.[101] Rape often has a (twisted) value component. You value your own needs more than your victim. You want to teach someone a lesson. You want to feel powerful. You feel you deserve to humiliate someone. All these values and emotions only apply to other people. We don't usually feel the urge to humiliate objects. It's precisely because someone is a human being that it matters how you treat him or her.

Paul Bloom wrote in the *New Yorker* about Fiske and Tage's analysis:

> *In many instances, violence is neither a cold-blooded solution to a problem nor a failure of inhibition; most of all, it doesn't entail a blindness to moral considerations. On the contrary, morality is often a motivating force ... Moral violence, whether reflected in legal sanctions, the killing of enemy soldiers in war, or punishing someone for an ethical transgression, is motivated by the recognition that its victim is a moral agent, someone fully human.* [102]

The men who raped me were very clear that they were angry at me. Don't ask me to explain why, and they're not available for comment. I just know that they were enraged. I had no right to be out with a boy, they said. They would teach me a lesson. This is what happens to bad girls. At no time was I just an object. At worst, I was a whore who had to be put in her place. At best, I was a fool who had to be taught a lesson. But I was definitely a *person.*

I babbled like a parakeet on speed through the whole ordeal, trying to get them to show some mercy. Talking about myself and my life and trying to get them to see me as worthy of compassion—all that went nowhere. I was a wicked, clueless girl and had to be taught. But one thing did have an effect—when I started talking about *them.* "We are all brothers and sisters," I ranted. "You are my brothers." That infuriated them. They didn't want to be reminded of their humanity.

This is just one story. But I think it's worth considering the idea that other rapists have equally distorted views of themselves and their victims.

Audrey, the young British woman who was gang-raped in Italy, told me that one of her rapists said in his police statement that he didn't need to rape to get women; he was so naturally attractive that women just flocked to him. In his mind, it wasn't even rape. She was just lying there, clearly fine with it, so what was the problem?

We've got a long way to go when we can't even agree on what is rape. Audrey went on to say that the judge in her case sided with the rapists. "The judge and prosecutor seemed to share this perspective to an extent—that rape was something only real psychos jumping out of bushes did, or losers who couldn't get sex any other way; it was not something that good-looking, well-dressed young men needed to resort to. I guess I would respond today that rape is really not about sexual attraction or having sex in the first place. Especially when you're talking about a group, there's a different dynamic at play, one that is more about humiliating someone and treating her as inferior … at least, this is the conclusion I have reached."

Consider the Stanford rape case. Undergraduate Brock Turner sexually assaulted an intoxicated woman and left her unconscious. A woman friend of his wrote a letter to the judge, which said, "Where do we draw the line and stop worrying about being politically correct every second of the day and see that rape on campuses isn't always because people are rapists?"

Rape on campus is always because people are rapists. We just don't want to think about the uncomfortable truth that a rapist is just a guy, any guy, who rapes.

"Does anyone enjoy raping?" Kalki Koechlin wanted to know when we were trying to figure it all out. "What's going on?"

Patriarchy is to blame, says writer bell hooks.

Provocative women are to blame, say the Iranian morality police.

Alcohol is to blame, says the Campus Sexual Assault Study, prepared for the US National Institute of Justice.[103] The woman who was raped by Brock Turner, the Stanford student who infamously got a ridiculously light sentence for his crime (from Santa Clara County Superior Court Judge Aaron Persky, who lost his position two years later), wrote a powerful letter to be read out in court. She talked about alcohol:

> *Alcohol is not an excuse. Is it a factor? Yes. But alcohol was not the one who stripped me, fingered me, had my head dragging against the ground, with me almost fully naked. Having too much to drink was an amateur mistake that I admit to, but it is not criminal. Everyone in this room has had a night where they have regretted drinking too much, or knows someone close to them who has had a night where they have regretted drinking too much. Regretting drinking is not the same as regretting sexual assault. We were both drunk; the difference is, I did not take off your pants and underwear, touch you inappropriately, and run away. That's the difference.* [104]

Brock Turner's father also wrote a letter about his son, to the judge. It is a devastating testament to rape culture:

> *Now he barely consumes any food and eats only to exist. These verdicts have broken and shattered him and our family in so many ways. His life will never be the one that he dreamed about and worked so hard to*

> *achieve. That is a steep price to pay for twenty minutes*
> *of action out of his twenty-plus years of life.*

Some rapists have permission to take what they want. Some rapists have had terrible lives full of abuse and despair. As a friend who was raped by a troubled man said, "You get a lot of shit on your plate—it starts to affect you." It's not an excuse, but a reality, like witnesses of domestic abuse who grow up to beat their partners. But then, there are the men who've had perfectly healthy, wholesome lives and commit rape anyway. What about them? Or the men who abuse their power, like those I've talked about in Washington, and Hollywood, whose penises have spent an inordinate amount of time outside their owners' pants.

It's time to throw one idiotic notion overboard—the notion that men can't stop, that there's a point of no return once you're sexually aroused. We keep talking about women's agency, but men have agency too. Guys, tell me this: if you were in the middle of hot sex and really, really into it, and your grandmother walked into the room and peered at you over her glasses, would you stop, or would you keep going?

Rape is like a go-to hobby for men of all types. Godmen in Goa.[105] Daddies in Denmark. Teachers in Tanzania. Boyfriends in Britain. Ski instructors in Switzerland. Priests in Prague.

This doesn't necessarily contradict my earlier point about rapists dehumanizing themselves. Violence has so many motivations. There's damage rape (you want to cause pain) and there's casual rape (you want sex).

When you look around at the whole panorama, it's difficult to muster up wholesale abhorrence of all abusers.

They're so aggravatingly human. So few have bulging red eyes, uncontrollable drooling, and fifteen heads. A therapist told me about how he took on the case of a fourteen-year-old boy who had raped a twelve-year-old autistic girl. "Everyone at the clinic thought he was a monster, and nobody wanted to take the case." The therapist wondered how he would deal with this twisted teenager. "And then, this sweet young kid walked in." He had been terribly sexually abused and brutalized himself, all his life, and he was "doing the only thing he knew."

Why they do it is interesting, but after a point I'm more interested in moving along from this unevolved state of human interaction. I don't want to care about rapists' motivations. They should just stop. Whether it's wired in or because their daddy didn't play with them or they're just jerks or they're sexually frustrated or they do it because they can or they do it because they can't not do it or they're normal or they're abnormal, who cares? They should just stop what one superior babysitter once called this "third-class behavior."

Unfortunately we do have to spend time trying to understand, if we're going to stop it. So yeah, we can't talk about rape without talking about why men rape.

28

A brief pause for terror

I AM WALKING on the beach at sunset. I could be blindfolded and still make my way home, I know the curve of this place so well. Like most of my cousins, I've been coming here since before I was born. It is our true home. Right now, I'm alone and content. The sun is setting and it is all no less beautiful for being a complete cliché—the sea, the setting sun, the almost-full moon rising gloriously behind the casuarina trees, parakeets shrieking in the distance. I glance over at the tree-line and see a man cutting wood, no big deal.

A few minutes later, I casually glance behind me. He's still there, a much smaller figure now, and I can't hear his axe any more. It's all peaceful and I remind myself that I'm having a serene evening walk. He probably didn't even notice me. I keep going.

There's no reason to look back, but I just happen to. Hmm. He's not there. Must have gone home. I do not have to look backwards again. I keep walking.

After they were through, the men who raped me and wounded my friend and me escorted us down the mountain. It might sound crazy, but they offered and we accepted—we were too hurt and lost to find our way down by ourselves in the dark. Once we reached the dirt road, they let us go, but then they followed us for a long time. This was possibly the most frightening part of the whole ordeal. I was convinced they were just toying with us, and waiting to run up and finally finish us off. For years afterwards, I couldn't stand the sound of footsteps behind me, or even the thought that someone might be there. This is highly inconvenient when you live in Bombay or New York. But those days are long gone, and now I'm fine. I'm fine, I'm fine, I'm *fine*.

I casually glance again. Now the sun is gone, and everything is darkening. Did something move among the trees? Why isn't anyone else in the family out for a walk?

The beach is perfectly peaceful and beautiful. The moon sails enigmatically on. I picture that man stalking me from the tree-line, quietly keeping pace with me, and calculating the exact moment he should break cover, come racing down the beach, jump on me, and ruin my life.

Dammit, this is my walk. Nothing's going to happen. It would be stupid to speed up and give in to paranoia. Stupid to surrender to creeping madness.

I speed up.

I start to jog a bit. I roll my eyes at myself. I almost fall down, suddenly overcome by a rush of sheer terror. It slams into me with a ferocity that feels physical. The whole world vibrates with menace. The friendly trees are monsters, the sea is acid purple and the moon a relentless spotlight that will find me no matter where I go. I run like hell and stop only when I see lights in one of my aunts' houses on the way.

Then I stop and casually stroll home. The moon is gorgeous again, the night once more soft and lovely.

29

The full catastrophe

I meant to write about death, only life came breaking in as usual.

— Virginia Woolf, diary entry,
17 February 1922

WHEN I WAS thirteen years old, my younger brother and I went on a trip during which someone gave us two large sarus crane eggs. We brought them home, and presented them to our father with full faith that he would hatch them. And he did. The crane who survived, Haty, lived with us for years. From the first day when she emerged as a golden ball of fluff, she imprinted on my father. He was her parent, her partner, her everything. When she was full-grown and almost as tall as us, Haty and he would whoop and call to each other, and race back and forth across the garden, flapping their wings in a wild mock mating dance.

What is this story doing in a book about rape? Isn't it obvious? Here is madness and magic in the world, here is the possibility of understanding across species, so why not within species? Here is the possibility of connection, of kindness, of illogical love.

When Manassah Bradley walks into a room to give a talk, he often begins by saying, "Hi, I'm Manassah. I was raped, and I'm happy. I'm not happy that I was raped, but I'm happy."

He explained to me that it's very important for him to do this. He went through years of pain, gave up on having children because he felt he wasn't whole enough, spent thousands of dollars on therapy, and now his life is good.

"When you hear people talk about rape, they say, 'Oh, my God, his life is ruined,'" he told me. "Who wants to hear that?"

I know just what he means. Everyone pays a price, but not everyone gets to come out the other end with some measure of joy.

Life exalts us, and life damages us. Some people are destroyed by rape; most are not. They come through it, they go on, wearing with great dignity a mantle of bitter grace. But they shouldn't have to. And they certainly shouldn't have to do it alone.

My mother didn't want me to get a job as a rape crisis counselor after college. "Anything but that!" she said, worried that I would spiral downwards after successfully putting my experience behind me. I got the job anyway, and one of the best things about those years at the Women's Center was my mother. We all looked forward to her visits. She would drive up in the afternoon after work, and climb up the blue wooden steps, knitting in one hand, pound cake in the other. She made herself comfortable on the sofa while rape victims called, battered women appeared, the phone rang with one problem after the other, and the demented cat with furious eyes raced up and down the steps. She just sat and knitted. She was there, a benign witness. It's impossible to express what that meant to everyone there—someone who brought us cake and just sat there, knitting implacably against fear and horror and isolation. She was our witness.

Zorba the Greek called the totality of life "the full catastrophe." Dancing cranes, mango season, love, music, moonrise, decay, violence—all of it, the full catastrophe. Rape is part of it. But I cannot, will not, accept that it is inevitable. Rape is a choice. Rapists choose to rape. The rest of us choose how we react. I don't care if I'm a mad dreamer, but I think a world without rape is possible.

Yasmin El-Rifae's manuscript[106] has a description of members of her Cairo intervention group talking with people in the crowds in Tahrir Square. They know that they are talking to potential sexual abusers, and to people who might not be willing to help even if they aren't rapists themselves. The group's tactic was to assume that people ultimately want to help, not hurt. This is a Q&A with Adam, a group member:

> *Do you remember when you figured this out?*
> *We always knew that people could be either/or.*
>
> *Because women themselves had said that people sometimes switched during the attacks?*
> *People just go crazy, they're encouraged by the others. But they could also want to be good people, with another social status. Do you want to be a harasser*

or do you want to be a hero? So we encouraged them to be heroes, by speaking with them very calmly, very intimately, speaking in their ear. Never adding to the sense of danger and hysteria by shouting or creating panic. We aimed to be a very quiet force, to allow people to come back to their senses in very small touches.

Did you find that difficult to do, to stay a peaceful presence?
You do it at a price, of course, because inside you're boiling and you're afraid. But you can only defuse madness and hysteria by being the exact opposite. It becomes almost weird, like, who is this block of ice in this fire, you know? It's the contrast that has effect.

It's like a performance.
Yes, completely. It's an act.

Except you're on the most terrifying stage.
It's like whispering into someone's ear at a death metal concert, and talking to them about Plato.

It's hard to make that leap of faith, that someone will choose to think about Plato at a death metal concert; choose to believe in true love with a crane; choose to help rather than harm. It's especially hard when history doesn't bear us out: our species' story is a story of rape and violation, on an individual as well as group level. It's hard to believe in people's innate humanity when you can go to a local shop in India and buy a rape video for a hundred rupees.

That's a real rape video, by the way, not a simulation. In North India, it's sometimes euphemistically called a "local video" or a "WhatsApp sex video."[107] You can go to a small general store and buy one for a pittance. Men rape women, film their actions, and then sell the videos.

I'd like to say that I have faith in human nature. Human nature is kindness and large-heartedness, compassion and respect. But human nature is also vile and cruel, selfish and entitled. I've been intimately engaged with all these sides of human nature, and I don't have an answer about what we really are. I do know that we make choices about how we treat each other, and too often the choice is to violate, to tear down and not build up. Does rape come from some primal instinct, or is it an inevitable outgrowth of the way we learn to relate to one another? Are we ever going to figure it out, together? No matter what the answer is, we certainly won't find it if we don't talk to each other.

In a world full of noise, it's easy to overlook the silence around rape. It's easier to talk about statistics and lofty principles than to try to wrestle with issues of impunity and unpredictable memory and illogical justifications; of shame and guilt and the tedium of a trauma that goes on and on and on. Of weird paradoxes that you can't easily categorize. I hope that all the voices in this book, from Ramallah to Copenhagen to Mumbai to Port Elizabeth, help to end some of the silence, illuminate some of the shadows.

Rape. Redemption. The full catastrophe.

Notes

1 Introduction

1 www.slate.com/blogs/the_slatest/2016/10/07/donald_trump_2005_tape_i_grab_women_by_the_pussy.html

2 https://transequality.org/sites/default/files/docs/usts/USTS-Executive-Summary-Dec17.pdf

2 Who am I to talk?

3 www.youtube.com/watch?v=c6sxzOpHQrY

4 www.nytimes.com/2013/01/08/opinion/after-being-raped-i-was-wounded-my-honor-wasnt.html

3 Shut up or die, crazy bitch

5 "Be warned."

6 Dept of Justice, Office of Justice Programs, Bureau of Justice Statistics, National Crime Victimization Survey, 2010–14 (2015)

7 http://journals.sagepub.com/doi/10.1177/1077801210387749

8 Slepian, M. L., J. S. Chun, and M. F. Mason (2017). The experience of secrecy. *Journal of Personality and Social Psychology*, 113(1), 1–33.; http://psycnet.apa.org/record/2017-20428-001

9 Beard, Mary, *Women & Power: A Manifesto*, Profile Books, London, 2017

10 www.bbc.com/news/entertainment-arts-41594672

11 http://news.bbc.co.uk/2/hi/africa/8650112.stm

12 www.panzifoundation.org/panzi-hospital

13 www.theguardian.com/world/2016/aug/03/kavumu-village-39-young-girls-raped-justice-drc

14 www.alternet.org/human-rights/how-one-american-journalist-took-down-militiamen-who-raped-50-young-girls

4   Totally different, exactly the same

15   www.dissentmagazine.org/article/breaking-cage-india-feminism-sexual-violence-public-space

16   www.scribd.com/document/121920147/Justice-J-S-Verma-committee-report-on-sexual-assault

17   www.bbc.com/news/magazine-38796457

18   www.amnestyusa.org/issues/death-penalty/death-penalty-facts

19   www.livemint.com/Leisure/NvPjEMDihrmOiL7XAjl6MP/Why-the-Delhi-sentence-is-too-much-and-too-little.html

20   www.washingtonpost.com/local/social-issues/calls-to-rape-crisis-centers-are-surging-amid-the-outpouring-of-sexual-assault-allegations/2017/11/22

21   https://people.com/archive/no-town-without-pity-a-divided-new-bedford-seeks-justice-in-a-brutal-gang-rape-case-vol-21-no-10

22   www.justice.gov/ovw/tribal-affairs

23   www.stuff.co.nz/national/21913/Abuse-of-Maori-women-shocking

24   www.aihw.gov.au/reports/domestic-violence/family-domestic-sexual-violence-in-australia-2018/contents/summary

25   www.ncdsv.org/images/SexAssaultandPeoplewithDisabilities.pdf

26   www.nytimes.com/2018/02/04/opinion/metoo-law-legal-system.html?mtrref=www.google.com&assetType=opinion

5   Yes, no, maybe

27   www.youtube.com/watch?v=oQbei5JGiT8

28   www.bbc.com/news/world-us-canada-41699245

29   Seager, Joni, *The Penguin Atlas of Women in the World*, 4th ed., Penguin Books, UK, 2009. pp.58–9

30   www.aljazeera.com/indepth/opinion/2017/08/middle-east-roll-repeal-marry-rapist-laws-170822095605552.html

31   www.bbc.com/news/entertainment-arts-41594672

32   www.buzzfeed.com/katiejmbaker/meet-the-expert-witness-who-says-sex-in-a-blackout-isnt?

33   www.slate.com/articles/news_and_politics/interrogation/2017/09/in_search_of_a_new_standard_for_sexual_consent_on_campus.html

34   www.vox.com/first-person/2018/1/19/16907246/sexual-consent-educator-aziz-ansari

35   www.bustle.com/p/who-is-madhumita-pandey-the-research-student-interviewed-over-100-convicted-rapists-in-india-heres-what-she-learned-2335827

36   www.vox.com/first-person/2018/1/19/16907246/sexual-consent-educator-aziz-ansari

37   www.nytimes.com/2017/08/05/us/usc-rape-case-dropped-video-evidence.html

6   What did you expect?

38   www.alternet.org/news-amp-politics/montana-lawyer-argues-13-year-old-rape-victim-blame-being-temptress

39   *Strong Island*, directed by Yance Ford, Yanceville Films, 2017. 1 hour, 13 minutes, 2 seconds into the film

40   http://mashable.com/2017/09/21/its-on-us-consent-logic-video

41   www.hrw.org/news/2013/07/03/egypt-epidemic-sexual-violence

7   Oh, please

42   www.detroitnews.com/story/tech/2018/01/18/msu-president-told-nassar-complaint-2014/1042071001
     www.nbcnews.com/news/us-news/olympic-committee-was-told-2015-suspected-abuse-nassar-n843786

43   www.mlive.com/news/index.ssf/2018/01/nassar_victim_describes_tellin.html

44   www.detroitnews.com/story/news/local/michigan/2017/11/22/larry-nassar-sexual-assault-charges/107934168

45   www.worldcrunch.com/opinion-analysis/full-translation-of-french-anti-metoo-manifesto-signed-by-catherine-deneuve

46   www.nytimes.com/2018/01/12/opinion/catherine-deneuve-french-feminists.html

47   www.odoxa.fr/sondage/plus-dune-femme-deux-france-a-deja-ete-victime-de-harcelement-dagression-sexuelle/

48   www.washingtonpost.com/blogs/compost/wp/2018/01/13/ladies-lets-be-reasonable-about-metoo-or-nothing-will-ever-be-sexy-again

8   How to save a life

49   www.timeslive.co.za/news/south-africa/2017-10-10-lion-mama-walks-free-after-fatal-stabbing

50 www.deccanchronicle.com/nation/crime/230917/chandigarhhc-suspends-sentences-of-3-convicts-accuses-girls-promiscuous-attitude.html

51 www.cnn.com/2017/07/27/asia/pakistan-revenge-rape/index.html

52 www.nytimes.com/2012/05/10/nyregion/ultra-orthodox-jews-shun-their-own-for-reporting-child-sexual-abuse.html

53 https://forward.com/news/308681/25-years-later-manny-waks-is-on-a-quest-to-confront-his-abuser/?attribution=tag-article-listing-1-headline

54 www.nytimes.com/2012/05/10/nyregion/ultra-orthodox-jews-shun-their-own-for-reporting-child-sexual-abuse.html

10   The official version

55 www.rainn.org/statistics/criminal-justice-system

56 http://news.trust.org/item/20180206171511-j0mac

57 UNDP *Editorial Style Guide,* 2014

11   Your love is killing me

58 https://babe.net/2018/01/13/aziz-ansari-28355

59 www.jaclynfriedman.com/unscrewed

60 www.vox.com/first-person/2018/1/19/16907246/sexual-consent-educator-aziz-ansari

12   A brief pause for horror

61 www.nytimes.com/2017/07/27/world/middleeast/isis-yazidi-women-rape-iraq-mosul-slavery.html

13   A bagful of dentures

62 www.nimh.nih.gov/health/topics/post-traumatic-stress-disorder-ptsd/index.shtml

63 www.ptsd.va.gov/professional/trauma/other/sexual_assault_against_females.asp

64 http://zaksdental.com.au

65 www.bostonglobe.com/metro/2018/02/06/jamaica-tufts-dentists-provide-care-for-rural-communities/vbWDFGnODY0UBI9glyZ5wO/story.html

66   www.ncbi.nlm.nih.gov/pmc/articles/PMC3096184/#i1524-5012-10-1-38-Little1

67   http://nautil.us/blog/when-cancer-treatment-re_traumatizes-survivors-of-sexual-trauma

14 Teflon Man

68   www.propublica.org/article/false-rape-accusations-an-unbelievable-story

69   http://dynamic.uoregon.edu/jjf/articles/freyd97r.pdf

70   www.rollingstone.com/music/news/taylor-swift-talks-groping-trial-sexual-assault-w513445

71   https://harpers.org/archive/2018/01/cant-touch-this

15 Keys to the kingdom

72   www.nytimes.com/2016/10/08/us/donald-trump-tape-transcript.html

73   http://abcnews.go.com/International/silvio-berlusconi-wiretaps-prime-minister-spare-time/story?id=14546921

74   www.pulse.ng/bi/lifestyle/the-15-beautiful-wives-that-king-mswati-iii-has-married-id7546888.html

75   www.slate.com/blogs/the_slatest/2016/10/07/donald_trump_2005_tape_i_grab_women_by_the_pussy.html

76   http://riceinstitute.org/blog/what-fraction-of-sexual-violence-in-india-is-within-marriages-media-coverage-of-research-by-aashish-gupta

77   www.thehindu.com/news/national/criminalising-marital-rape-will-destabilise-marriage-govt-tells-hc/article19581512.ece

78   www.rappler.com/nation/politics/elections/2016/129784-viral-video-duterte-joke-australian-woman-rape

79   https://zimbabwe-today.com/grace-mugabe-women-who-wear-mini-skirts-deserve-to-be-raped-southafrica-zimbabwe-nigeria-robertmugabe

80   http://aids-freeworld.org/Publications-Multimedia/Reports/Electing-to-Rape.aspx?view=web_report

17 Rx—polite conversation

81   www.theguardian.com/commentisfree/2013/apr/26/protect-children-talk-rape-desmond-tutu

82   Enloe, Cynthia, *The Big Push: Exposing and Challenging the Persistence of Patriarchy*, Myriad Editions, Oxford, 2017. p.49

83   www.reddit.com/r/MuseumOfReddit/comments/1t1r2z/the_ask_a_rapist_thread

84   http://answer.rutgers.edu/blog/2015/06/12/sex-education-must-work-to-dismantle-rape-culture

20   Stealing freedom, stealing joy

85   www.mosac.net/page/285

86   https://medium.com/skin-stories/when-secrets-turn-into-stories-living-with-ptsd-as-a-young-queer-woman-146f49f2a4a5

87   https://storage.googleapis.com/vera-web-assets/downloads/Publications/overlooked-women-and-jails-report/legacy_downloads/overlooked-women-and-jails-report-updated.pdf

22   A brief pause for ennui

88   Haupt, Lyanda Lynn, *Mozart's Starling*, Little, Brown and Company, New York, 2017

22   The quality of mercy

89   Elva, Thordis and Tom Stranger, *South of Forgiveness*, Scribe Publications, Victoria, Australia, 2017; and Skyhorse Publishing, New York, 2017

90   www.ted.com/talks/thordis_elva_tom_stranger_our_story_of_rape_and_reconciliation

91   www.cnn.com/2018/02/05/us/larry-nassar-sentence-eaton/index.html

24   Your rape is worse than mine

92   De Guissmé, Laura, and Laurent Licata (2017). "Competition over collective victimhood recognition: When perceived lack of recognition for past victimization is associated with negative attitudes towards another victimized group." *European Journal of Social Psychology*, 47: 148–166. https://doi: 10.1002/ejsp.2244

93   www.inanna.ca/catalog/im-girl-who-was-raped

94   www.theweek.in/content/archival/news/india/dont-criminia lise-marital-rape-violence-not-just-forcible-sexual-penetration-flavia-agnes.html

25 Good girls don't

95 www.vice.com/en_us/article/evvm7e/grandmothers-in-nairo bi-are-fighting-off-rapists-with-self-defense-techniques-v24n7

96 www.nytimes.com/2018/01/20/style/confronting-sexual-harassment-dominatrix-training.html

97 www.aidsdatahub.org/sites/default/files/documents/new/Rights-Evidence-Report-2015-final.pdf

98 www.livemint.com/Leisure/pf20TksLBZSZ3jtFR7oLSP/Sex-work-and-violence.html

99 www.melissaditmore.com

100 www.sangram.org/resources/RAIDED-E-Book.pdf

27 Boys will...

101 Fiske, Alan Page, and Tage Shakti Rai, *Virtuous Violence: Hurting and Killing to Create, Sustain, End, and Honor Social Relationships*, Cambridge University Press, Cambridge, 2014

102 www.newyorker.com/magazine/2017/11/27/the-root-of-all-cruelty

103 www.ncjrs.gov/pdffiles1/nij/grants/221153.pdf

104 www.theguardian.com/us-news/2016/jun/06/stanford-sexual-assault-case-victim-impact-statement-in-full

105 www.alternet.org/world/mob-violence-india-will-have-legal-repercussions-once

29 The full catastrophe

106 www.yasminelrifae.com

107 www.aljazeera.com/indepth/features/2016/10/dark-trade-rape-videos-sale-india-161023124250022.html

Index

Original sources and permissions

What We Talk About When We Talk About Love by Raymond Carver. Copyright © 1993, Tess Gallagher, used by permission of Tess Gallagher.

"What We Talk About When We Talk About Love," copyright © 1981 by Raymond Carver; from *What We Talk About When We Talk About Love* by Raymond Carver. Used by permission of Alfred A. Knopf, an imprint of the Knopf Doubleday Publishing Group, a division of Penguin Random House LLC. All rights reserved. Any third party use of this material, outside of this publication, is prohibited. Interested parties must apply directly to Penguin Random House LLC for permission.

Thank you to Verlyn Klinkenborg for permission to quote from *The Rural Life*, Little, Brown, New York, 2002.

Thanks to Leslee Udwin for permission to quote from her film *India's Daughter*, 2015.

Grateful thanks to Profile Books for permission to quote from *Women & Power, a Manifesto*, © 2017 Mary Beard, Profile Books, London.

Pan Macmillan gave permission to use the quote from *Last Bus to Woodstock*, © 1975 Colin Dexter, Pan Books, London.

Thanks to Vanessa Grigoriadis, for letting me quote from her interview in *Slate* magazine.

Yance Ford generously let me quote from his film *Strong Island*, Yanceville Films, 2017.

Tarzan of the Apes. Published in the UK by Gollancz, 2012. © 1912 Edgar Rice Burroughs, Inc.

Vakils Publications kindly allowed me to quote from *Cooking Delights of the Maharajas*, © 1982 Digvijaya Singh, Vakils, Feffer & Simons Ltd., Mumbai.

I am grateful to Cynthia Enloe for her quote from *The Big Push*, © Cynthia Enloe 2017, Myriad Editions, Oxford.

"Chapter 20" from *Bastard Out of Carolina* by Dorothy Allison, copyright © 1992 by Dorothy Allison. Used by permission of Dutton, an imprint of Penguin Publishing Group, a division of Penguin Random House LLC. All rights reserved.

Thordis Elva generously granted permission for me to quote from *South of Forgiveness*, © 2017 Thordis Elva and Tom Stranger, Skyhorse Publishing, New York.

I am honored and grateful that the author allowed me to quote from his novel *The Yellow Birds*, © Kevin Powers 2012, Sceptre, London.

I am immensely grateful to Yasmin el-Rifae for sharing her story and perspective with me, and generously letting me enhance my book with some of the best sections of hers.

Acknowledgements

Thank you for saving my life:

Aalia Abdulali. Shumoon Abdulali. Adil Abdulali. I hit the jackpot with you three. Tom Unger, superhero who cooked, edited, researched, encouraged, laughed, tolerated, understood, brought home the bacon and pomegranates and gnomes. Samara Unger, seed with wings. Geoffrey Alperin. Ráshid Ali. Aziza Tyabji Hydari. Sheila Naharwar. Bishakha Datta. Susan Hamburger. Sophie Molholm. Janet Yassen and the women of the Boston Area Rape Crisis Center.

Thank you for helping this become a book:

I'm incredibly lucky to have a posse of international publishers, led by four fantastic feminist editors.

Myriad Editions, UK: Candida Lacey began it all. She is outrageously wonderful: fierce, loyal, and ridiculously smart. Life without our regular Skype gossip session is a morose prospect indeed. And thank you also to Linda McQueen who is to manuscripts what Michelangelo was to marble. Thank you to the rest of the team: Dawn Sackett, Isobel McLean, Corinne Pearlman, Emma Dowson, Anna Burtt, Anna Morrison, Louisa Pritchard. Thanks, too, to

Dan Raymond-Barker and all at New Internationalist, Myriad's publishing partners, who believed in this book from its very early pages.

Penguin/Random House India: Manasi Subramaniam, thank you for insisting that *this* was the book to write.

Penguin/Random House Australia/New Zealand: Meredith Curnow, thank you for the excellent suggestions and the badass orange tote bag. Thank you, Sarah Hayes.

The New Press, USA: Ellen Adler, thank you for reading my book in bad light on your phone on a plane, leaping into action, and ignoring all publishing protocol. Thank you to Brian Ulicky, Sarah Swong, and everyone else at The New Press for being so committed to the book. Thanks are also due to McLean Peña and Daniella Roseman for their careful reading of the final manuscript.

Also in the US: thank you for your enthusiasm and generosity in spreading the word, Sarah McNally of McNally Jackson Books and Angela Baggetta of Angela Baggetta Communications.

Thank you for your input, wisdom, time, and research help:

Yasmin El-Rifae. Irene Metter. Bishakha Datta. Cynthia Enloe. Harlyn Aizley. Kalki Koechlin. Mitali Ayyangar and Médecins Sans Frontières. Laila Atshan. Meena Seshu and SANGRAM. Nomawethu Siswana, Jana Zindell and Ubuntu Pathways. Sean Grover. Jaclyn Friedman. Christopher Mario. Siddharth Dube. Sharonne Zaks. Tina Horn. Sami Faltas. Gina Scaramella. Melissa Ditmore. Geeta Misra. Tom Unger again. Tom Unger again.

Thank you for talking with me:

The people who generously shared their stories with me have been through crazy hell and most have put themselves back together with grace and spirit. Some have not – everyone's story isn't a triumphant one. We used up quite a few tissues while talking, but we also had a good giggle or two. What a privilege to spend time with you warriors and heroes. I wish I could put all your names up in neon.

About the author

Sohaila Abdulali was born in Mumbai. She has a BA from Brandeis University in economics and sociology and an MA from Stanford University in communication. She is the author of two novels as well as children's books and short stories. She lives in New York with her family.

31901063932976